Acclaim for
SUPER YOU

Super You wisely begins by grounding the spiritual practitioner in the rich soil of loving kindness towards oneself. Epstein then goes the length in revealing that the super hero within each of us is already fully equipped to rise victorious amid all of life's challenges and live our highest potential as spiritual beings having a human incarnation.

— Michael Bernard Beckwith, Author of *Life Visioning*

"*Super You* is a wonderful book that shows you how to tap into your amazing powers for success, happiness, and inner peace."

—Brian Tracy, author of *No Excuses!:*
The Power of Self-Discipline

Super You offers a clear and wise guide to the seven essential ingredients of the spiritual path. It both enlightens and inspires.

—Marci Shimoff, *NY Times* bestselling author of *Happy for No Reason* and featured teacher in the film, *The Secret*

We are drinking from the same well. Knowing *Super You* is the true purpose of life.

—Jim Rosemergy, former Executive Vice President of Unity School of Christianity and author of *A Closer Walk with God*

"*Super You* is very practical, and needed by most people. Justin does a great job closing the gap between our humanity and our divinity."

—Walter Starcke, former Broadway producer and author of *The Double Thread*

"*Super You* is a refreshing breath of air that will inspire you, release you, and give you the tools to uncover the amazing golden core of you."

—Liah Kraft-Kristaine, author of *30 Days to Happiness: Setting Yourself Up to Win in Life*

"I'm amazed, awed, and impressed by how Justin skillfully blends, and integrates abstract spiritual principles with many down-to-earth examples the reader can identify with. *Super You* is very reader-friendly and compelling. Each chapter is full of practical tips that people can immediately apply to their lives."

—Dr. Michael Klausner, associate professor of sociology, University of Pittsburgh at Bradford

"I thoroughly enjoyed reading *Super You* and will share it with a friend."

—Wally "Famous" Amos, entrepreneur, author, speaker, philanthropist

I love *Super You*. Each chapter takes me somewhere. It is simple with lots of depth and easy to read, absorb, and understand. I have much more compassion for others and myself as a result. Justin is able to communicate forgiveness and letting go in a tangible and practical way, which very few authors are able to do.

—Elle B. Willson, singer and songwriter

"Justin Epstein sees the 'Super You' as the spiritual self, the place where God is expressed as you. Epstein provides clear, detailed descriptions of the principles and practices that enable one to awaken spiritually and to experience the divine inner self. Included are useful exercises that facilitate this process. This book will be helpful, not only for those who are new to Unity, but for traditional Christians who are searching for more effective ways to connect with the God-presence within them."

> —Neal Vahle, author of *The Unity Movement: Its Evolution and Spiritual Teaching,* and *The Spiritual Journey of Charles Fillmore: Discovering the Power Within*

"Nicely done and informative."

> —Roy Eugene Davis, author of *Paramahansa Yogananda As I Knew Him*, founder and spiritual director, Center for Spiritual Awareness

"Written in a delightfully warm, yet highly practical style, Justin's wisdom, insight and teachings set before the reader a clear and inviting path to spiritual growth that, if practiced, will not disappoint."

> —Rev. Wendy Craig-Purcell, author of *Ask Yourself This: Questions to Open the Heart, Expand the Mind and Awaken the Soul*

"There is no doubt in my mind that your book will reach the multitude and help many people realize their divine potentials. I salute you for who you are and what you do."

> —Beth Leilani Mercado Ph.D. , author of *Whispers of the Soul*

Anne Murphy,

SUPER YOU

7 Steps to
Profound Peace
and Personal Power

Justin Epstein

Wishing you God's
richest blessings,

Justin Epstein

Cover Design by George Foster
Interior Design by Cypress House

ISBN: 978-0-9779310-5-7

Library of Congress Control Number: 2007900907

Printed in the USA

2 4 6 8 9 7 5 3 1

First edition

This book is dedicated to my parents:
My mom, Constance Rich
My stepfather, Henry Linkus
My late father, Robert Epstein
I love you.

Contents

Acknowledgments

To my family whose love and support throughout the years is deeply appreciated: Mom and Henry; Jonathan, brother; Ron, brother in spirit; Elana and Roxanne, sisters; Elizabeth, niece; James, nephew; and Aunt Nancy.

To my dear friends—you are shining lights.

Thanks to those in the following spiritual communities who were a part of the discovery and communication of the ideas in *Super You*:

Unity Church, Hilton Head Island, South Carolina

Unity Center, New York City

Unity Church, Tidewater, Virginia

Ananda Sangha communities

Thanks to John Niendorff, Andrea Sonia, Robin Quinn, Melanie Rigney, and most especially to Sal Glynn for editorial assistance and advice.

Thanks to my spiritual mentors: Rev. Eric Butterworth, Rev. Joyce Kramer, Rev. Jim Rosemergy, Rev. Wendy Craig Purcell, Joel Goldsmith, Swami Kriyananda, Paramhansa Yogananda, Swami Satchidananda, Dr. Wayne Dyer, Leo Buscaglia, Dr. Robert Schuller, and Dr. Norman Vincent Peale.

Special appreciation to those who read parts or the entire manuscript in its many versions, gave feedback and support, or whose story is included in *SuperYou*: Wally "Famous" Amos, Dr. Maya Angelou, Kimberley Ashley, Pat Bell, Eric Butterworth, Alan Cohen, Beatrice Crawford, Roy Eugene Davis, Ed Dodge, Jon Douillard, Rachel Edmond, Nancy Ellis-Bell, Debra Englander, Susan Farwell, Joel Fotinos, Ron Fulcher, Rev. Edwene Gaines, Clara Galvano, Dorothy Grigg, Lillian Heyward, Susan James, Rod Kenney, Dr. Michael Klausner, Rev. Joyce Kramer, Jon Kremer, Swami Kriyananda, Patricia London, Rev. Cecilia B. Loving, Peggy McColl, Gloria Damita P. Mills, Debi Mulanax, Steven Peterson, Dan Poynter, Bill Roper, Larry Ryder, Rev. Jim Rosemergy, Swami Satchidananda, Scott Scioli, Andrea Sonia, Walter Starcke, Brian Tracy, Linda Warnoch, Don Weiss, Rev. Jo Williams, Elle B. Willson, Alexandra Zykova, and the 2009 small groups from Unity Church of Hilton Head Island.

Introduction
Your Super Potential

*"If we did all the things we are capable of doing,
we would literally astonish ourselves."*
—Thomas Alva Edison

The greatest things that happen in your life are not consciously thought about or planned, like meeting a special someone, reading a life-changing book, or getting a great job. These coincidences have to do with Super You, even though you may not know it. Through knowing your deepest, Spiritual Self, you can attain what you need to be truly happy without making jobs, relationships, health, and things the primary focus of your life.

What is Super You? What do we long for more than anything else? What will give us peace and happiness, and also whatever is necessary for our highest fulfillment?

Super You is the Spiritual Self, the place within where God is expressed as *you*. Your Spiritual Self is an expression of God like a wave is an expression of the ocean. The wave contains the same components as the ocean and yet is a unique manifestation.

Whatever you call the Universe—God, Spirit, Source, Jehovah, Father, Mother, Allah, Brahman, the Tao, or Great Spirit—this presence is everywhere and in everything, including you. You are Super You. Through knowing your true Self, you will discover your connection with the Universe and all that is in it. The Super You fulfills your highest purpose for living and is your greatest source of happiness.

When you know your connection with the Universe, you allow health, love, money, career, relationships, and other wonderful treasures to come into your life without making them the sole focus of your awareness. You discover a deep sense of meaning and purpose as well as inner peace, freedom, and contentment. *Super You* shows the seven steps for knowing your Spiritual Self and finding the peace that your soul longs for.

Throughout this book, I use the terms Universe, God, Source, and Spirit to refer to the intelligence or force that abides around and within us. The terms "Super You" and "Spiritual Self" refer to God expressed as you. By tapping into your inner potential, you can become the person you have always wanted to be.

When you stop looking outside of yourself for happiness, fulfillment, success, and abundance, and instead look within to your Spiritual Self, you will start living the life you were meant to live.

You may resist the idea of having more potential than you have yet experienced. Remember the caterpillar that looked up in the sky and seeing a butterfly, said: "You'll never get me up in one of those things." What we fear is not that we can't fly, but that we can. Our most profound fear is we can do anything, be anyone, and live more fully than we do now. We shade our eyes against the light, not the dark.

Furthermore, we have a specific mission on earth, which, in the process of completing, will give us a tremendous sense of fulfillment—the "something else" we search for. Viktor Frankl, psychiatrist and concentration-camp survivor, said: "Everyone has his own specific vocation or mission in life; everyone must carry out a concrete assignment that demands fulfillment. Therein he cannot be replaced, nor can his life be repeated. Thus, everyone's task is as unique as is his specific opportunity to implement it."

Our mission is to find God by accessing our Spiritual Self, and to give expression to this Self. This is our super mission. It is the very thing we are supposed to do with our life, using our unique gifts in a way that no one else can.

Raised Jewish in Virginia Beach, I attended Hebrew school through the sixth grade and received bar mitzvah in an orthodox synagogue. However, I was not particularly religious. I did pray at times as an eight year old: "Dear God, please don't let Mom or Dad or Henry die," and as a thirteen year old: "Dear God, please make that pretty blonde girl at the pool like me." Not only did she like me, she and her friend soon joined me in the living room of my parent's apartment. You'd think prayer would have been a bigger part of my life after that.

At the age of eighteen, I looked into a mirror and saw that the luster had gone from my eyes. I was a freshman at James Madison University in Northern Virginia and just a few months earlier had graduated from Norfolk Collegiate High School. I had served as president of the junior class and student government, captain of the wrestling and golf teams, and was given many awards on graduation. A friend referred to me as the BMOC, and then had to explain it meant "big man on campus." I took for granted that I had always been happy, self-confident, friendly, popular, and successful. And then things changed.

My first real romantic relationship had ended badly. I was attracted to females from a young age (at six I had hoped to receive one of those long kisses at the kissing booth at camp; a peck on the lips left me disappointed), and my first girlfriend, also at camp, lasted only four days. I gave her my canteen money, thinking that I was responsible for an alimony payment when we broke up. Though I liked girls, I was shy. I heeded my stepfather Henry's advice: "You'll have plenty of time for girls later on. Focus on your studies and sports." It wasn't until I was a senior in high school that I met Cindy. She asked me to the Sadie Hawkins dance and I asked her to Homecoming. From then on, we saw each other nearly every day. Though I cared for her and she for me, we fought a lot. I often followed her to find out what I had said or not said that triggered her sadness and anger. Soon I felt trapped and was very critical of Cindy in my thoughts. My personality changed. I started to become cynical and withdrawn.

That summer after graduating high school, I read *How to Win Friends and Influence People* by Dale Carnegie, wanting to be a better leader and communicator. Instead, I became over-analytical and self-conscious when interacting with people one on one. The anxiety spread to public speaking, which I had always done so easily. What had been my greatest strengths, my personality and communication skills, were a huge source of pain. Instead of making a great impression on people, I made a very negative one. At least that's how I saw it.

I was transforming, and like the caterpillar in the cocoon, I was no longer recognizable. Friends from high school who had showered me with love and affection looked at me with raised eyebrows and wondered, "What happened to Justin?"

In addition to the emotional challenges of my relationship with Cindy and the changes in my personality, I questioned the purpose of life. After my success in high school, I was burdened by having to do it all again in college. There had to be more than receiving awards, being popular, making good grades, and winning in sports. The life ahead of me seemed like a treadmill: "Be successful, make lots of money, marry, raise a family, grow old, retire, and die." What a drag. I experienced what the sage Paramhansa Yogananda referred to as "anguishing monotony." I was confused and lost.

In my search for answers to life's meaning and wanting to regain the happiness I once had, I picked up one of my mother's yoga books, back when yoga was not as well known as it is today. The book was *To Know Your Self* by Swami Satchidananda. Many Sundays while growing up, my stepfather Henry and I would return home from the golf course to a house filled with people chanting, "Hari Om. Hari Om. Hari. Hari. Hari Om." Henry would roll his eyes with a wry smile on his face as we tip toed to our respective rooms; he watched sports and I did homework. Then we joined Mom and her hippie-yogi friends in their Birkenstock sandals and ate vegetarian Indian food. We didn't take Mom's yoga activities seriously. We thought it was just one among the many other things she was involved in.

Fascinated by Satchidananda's book, I wondered whether his teachings were really the truth. I read books on philosophy, psychology, communication, and religion. I read the Bible and *Bhagavad Gita*, and many self-help books. I listened to motivational gurus, watched evangelist Robert H. Schuller's *Hour of Power* on television every Sunday morning, and attended churches and Christian groups. I frequented bookstores and listened to audiotapes of Wayne Dyer and Leo Buscaglia. Finally, I declared a double major in Religion/Philosophy and Interpersonal Communication at university.

My search continued for over twenty years. I went from the synagogues of Virginia to ministerial training in Missouri to living in two different ashrams, one in the foothills of Northern California, and working at the Unity Center of New York City with renowned author and speaker, Eric Butterworth. I asked questions of the top spiritual and self-development teachers in the world: Is God inside of me, and every person? Is Jesus the *only* way to God? Is peace and joy my true nature? Is the knowledge of God, my true Self, the primary purpose of my life? These were a few of the questions I asked. Gratefully, I found many answers.

I first learned about the Law of Attraction twenty-two years ago through the Unity Church, founded by Charles and Myrtle Fillmore in the late 1800s. The law says that whatever you think about, you will manifest in your life. This can be used for money, opportunities, relationships, and health, but the sages of East and West warn that no matter how much material wealth we obtain, we can never be completely satisfied until we fully experience our Spiritual Self.

Material desires are endless and the more we have, the more we want. We will not be completely satisfied until we discover our Spiritual Self. I asked myself, "If thoughts create my life experience, what are the highest thoughts that I can possibly think?" With time and deep reflection, I realized that the highest thoughts were those that had to do with the Spiritual Self. The result of focusing attention on knowing the Spiritual Self is that I have had experiences far more wonderful than I could imagine. Through applying the steps in *Super You*, now I am a content, confident, peaceful, and happy person.

What I learned in my searching is that a great mystery exists that very few have completely realized through the ages. These people include Jesus, Moses, the Buddha, Krishna, Lao Tzu, and many others. Their message was that the purpose of life was to know the spiritual dimension of one's self, satisfying the deepest longing of the soul, an experience of one's true Self within and the source of infinite joy and peace. They taught that every person has the capacity to know their Spiritual Self. Most of their followers, however, have not understood their teaching. Instead, they worshipped the messengers, and the tools to attaining the Spiritual Self remained hidden.

Millions are now ready to learn what the sages tried to convey. We are no longer bound by the religion of our grandparents. We can cross the denominational lines to find the missing peace our souls hunger for. Those skeptical of organized religion are seeking a more spiritual way of life. This desire is evident in the popularity of such books as *A New Earth* by Eckhart Tolle and *The Secret* by Rhonda Byrne. As a Unity Church minister, I come into contact with many people from traditional Christianity that want more than theological terms and promises that have little to do with this life. They want more than to just read *about* God; they want to experience His presence of peace, joy, fulfillment, and success here and now. They want deeper answers to life's questions. They want a more direct relationship with Source.

Even when we are successful at getting what we want, we often fear losing it. Through knowing Super You, you will find contentment independent of outer things and still attract and enjoy them. You will feel more love than you ever thought possible, whether in a romantic relationship or not. Inner security comes independent of the economy or the balance of your checkbook because Super You is the source of all love and unlimited abundance.

Through applying the seven steps, I went from being confused, lost, and lethargic to having clarity, peace, satisfaction, calmness, joy, light-heartedness, and a sense of meaning and purpose. When you apply the seven steps, you will also experience whatever is necessary for your highest happiness.

The seven steps are the essence of my twenty-five years of research, study, daily meditation, and sincere seeking. Through understanding and applying these steps, your spiritual growth will take quantum leaps.

Henry David Thoreau said, "A truly good book teaches me better than to read it. I must soon lay it down, and commence living on its hint. What I began by reading, I must finish by acting." Many of us, as Eric Butterworth wrote, are over-read and underdone. It's more fun to obtain new information than it is to apply what we already know or are now learning. Applying what you learn is the only way to move beyond intellectual knowledge about spiritual principles to actually knowing them and experiencing their benefits.

Many people have a head full of spiritual principles or concepts, but struggle with the same problems. They know a lot *about* God and the Universe, but they don't possess a deep knowledge *of* God. Having faith involves going beyond intellectual belief to actual experience of Spirit. Instead of simply reading *Super You* and filling your head with intellectually stimulating ideas and uplifting stories, pause whenever you read an idea that touches you deeply, and think how you can apply the idea immediately to your life. The exercises at the end of each chapter support you in making the ideas and practices your own.

Read the book through once and then go back and reread one chapter per week or month, to deepen your understanding and application of the ideas. Keep *Super You* near your favorite reading spot so that you can easily return to it. Teach others what you learn; this will clarify the ideas in your own mind, accelerate your spiritual progress, and expose others to these life-transforming ideas and practices. The answers are within you. The book you hold in your hands will guide you to discovering those answers along with the peace, happiness, and fulfillment your heart craves.

You will also find true stories of people who have applied these steps with incredible results. The powerful and proven principles will take your spiritual life and experience of happiness and fulfillment to a whole new level.

It is my sincere hope that you will find peace, joy, success and spiritual fulfillment that thousands of others have found by applying the ideas and spiritual practices of *Super You*. If they have done it, you can too.

The master teacher, Jesus, said: "But rather seek ye the kingdom of God; and all these things shall be added unto you." (Luke 12:31) Become Super You by applying the seven steps for a spiritual breakthrough and watch everything else be added unto you.

Super You is more than just a book. For enhanced content, a free newsletter, additional support in meditation, or to attend a live presentation with Justin, scan the QR code below or log on to www.superyoubook.com/bookbonus. I would love to hear about how you have applied the principles from this book, or how they have blessed someone else.

Step One

Super Acceptance

*"Have patience with all things, but chiefly
have patience with yourself."*
—Saint Francis de Sales

Even Jesus struggled with his humanness. He wept at the death of his friend, Lazarus, and angrily ran the moneychangers out of the temple. He once refused to heal someone. In the Garden of Gethsemane the night prior to his crucifixion, Jesus sweated drops of blood and prayed that he wouldn't have to undergo the upcoming painful events. Saint Paul expressed his own conflicts between his human and Spiritual Self when he said: "I do not understand my own actions. For I do not do what I want, but I do the very thing I hate."

You and I also struggle with our human selves. For instance, we want to lose weight and promise to avoid high calorie foods and go to the gym more often. Instead, we open the freezer in the middle of the night and down a pint of Häagen-Dazs ice cream or let another day go by without exercise. One of the steps to expressing our Super You potential is embracing our humanness.

Susan reads a book of spiritual writings daily. There have been days when within an hour of reading a positive affirmation such as "I treat those I love with honor and respect" she has an argument with her husband. Have you ever left a church, spiritual center, synagogue, mosque, or temple feeling inspired, only to have a car pull out in front of you, leaving you angry and uttering less than holy words?

The following are suggestions for embracing your humanness in order to express Super You.

Don't Be An Ostrich

We sometimes try to ignore the unpleasantness of our human foibles. However, trying to pretend they don't exist will not make them disappear. Burying our heads in the sand only empowers the dreaded aspects of our self, and, as with the ostrich, exposes a certain part of our anatomy. Sooner or later, our unacknowledged and unwanted behaviors will bite us in that sensitive area. We're better off being conscious of our humanness rather than allow our foibles to have a negative impact.

For six years, I was more interested in finding answers to life's questions and determining a career than I was in how I related to people. In ministerial school I began to overcome my discomfort talking with people. Going to New York and serving as Eric Butterworth's associate made me realize I had to reach out in order to fulfill what God was calling me to do. I sought counseling, consulted communication experts, read books, and attended seminars on public speaking and one-on-one. A turning point came when I decided to be peaceful when interacting with people regardless of how I affected them, or how they perceived me. I loved myself anyway, despite the times I was anxious or awkward. I started to be more at ease and found answers to the dilemma. Today I am comfortable speaking to a group or interacting one-on-one. However, I am still committed to improvement in these areas, without the "paralysis by analysis." Learning communication skills is a must for people who want to live to the fullest and love people in the best way possible.

Only by choosing peace and to love myself did the healing begin. I made progress and as a result, am a wiser, gentler, and more thoughtful communicator. By facing my humanness and being persistent I overcame what held me back.

Unpleasant situations can enter our lives. "Yea, though I walk through the valley of the shadow of death..." (Psalm 23:4) implies that our entire earthly sojourn will not be rose-strewn. How we react to those situations is what counts.

One of the reasons we're afraid to see our human shortcomings is that we believe our behaviors define who we are as people. It's important to know that we are not our behaviors and **the situations in which we find ourselves are opportunities for soul growth** that we have chosen.

Through the Spiritual Self, we have the power to become conscious of our behaviors, which leads to the transformation of them. We are not our thoughts and emotions. We are spiritual beings who have thoughts, emotions, and behaviors.

❋ *Be aware of your thoughts, feelings, and behaviors without labeling them or yourself as good or bad. Read the list below and determine whether any of the items are good or bad. Test yourself at one-week intervals until you no longer attach such labels.*

❋ *Sexual fantasy while praying or meditating*

❋ *Cursing*

❋ *Anger at your child about what they said or did*

❋ *Criticizing another person*

❋ *Eating sweets*

❋ *Guilt after making an unkind remark*

❋ *Watching an adult movie*

❋ *Rejecting a request to serve on a committee*

❋ *Jealousy over how another person looks*

❋ *Sexually admiring a man or woman*

❋ *Fear over your finances*

❋ *Telling a lie*

❋ *Skipping your workout or meditation*

❋ *Late arrival at a meeting or an appointment*

❋ *Though these are not good or bad, acting on them may produce pain for yourself and others, and inhibit your growth and success. Be aware of what flows through you without judgment, and follow the path that is best for your highest growth and spiritual expression. Accept yourself in the moment and choose how you want to act and who you want to become.*

Love Rather Than Condemn Yourself

Are you unable to let go of mistakes? Do you torture yourself by replaying the scenes in your mind? Sometimes, guilt, regret, or a victim mentality can seem like acceptable ways to deal with a painful event. You think: "If only I had… I should have done … None of this is my fault…" However, feeling guilty or victimized can cause you to repeat the unwanted behavior. According to the Law of Attraction, what you focus upon with emotion, you tend to repeat. ***Realize that you have the choice to change an unwanted behavior without hurtful condemnation.*** Once you have done something you regret, instead of punishing yourself, resolve to learn from the experience and do better next time. Say to yourself: "Okay, it happened. Now what can I do about it?"

None of us will live perfectly no matter what lofty aspirations we have. We can only keep moving in the right direction. There was a time on the spiritual path when I was overly critical of myself. I believed that I needed to feel bad about my behavior to change it. My harsh attitudes blocked the experience of love that was always present within me. Only when I learned to love my flawed human self could I make the changes that I wanted. Remember that your Super Self is not a hanging judge, but rather a compassionate observer that lovingly supports your human self toward growth.

We create frustration when we expect to be perfect as we seek to be better. Instead of getting upset when you falter on your path, love and accept yourself right where you are and keep making the effort to get better. This is what Jesus meant when he said to the woman caught in adultery: "Neither do I condemn thee: go, and sin no more." (John 8:11)

Every person has an inborn desire for blossoming into the person he or she can become. Just as there is an invisible pattern within the acorn for the oak tree, there is a spiritual pattern within us for who we can become. We do not need to *make* ourselves spiritual beings; we just need to know and grow into it. When a crawling baby is learning to walk, nobody needs to tell him or her to get up and start walking. Super You nudges the baby to go ahead and get up on their feet. Parents give the baby encouragement, and would not dream of berating him or her for falling down. Similarly, offer your humanness that same kind of loving support, knowing that the desire to grow and transcend is inherent in each of us.

The Words

Don drove to his family home not long before his father's death, with the hope that his dad would tell him, "I love you." While driving back home and not hearing the words he longed for, Don realized that his father was incapable of saying these words to him. He decided to be a loving parent to himself.

Imagine an innocent child within you, full of love and good intentions. You can become the parent of this child, and even offer him or her the kind of parenting you wish you had received while growing up. The child will inevitably make mistakes, but you need not reject him or her. By having this kind of relationship with yourself, you can gradually chip away at self-criticism. Instead of waiting for others to give you love and approval, find it within yourself.

When I first spoke at Lincoln Center in New York City as the associate minister to Eric Butterworth, I was very critical of my Sunday messages and would sometimes be anxious and sad afterward. One day, I decided that no matter how I judged the speech to have gone, I was going to silently repeat, "I love myself." In this way, I kept a positive flow of love and joy within myself. I was finally able to separate my performance from how I felt about myself. I was able to love myself, learn from the experience, and then move on. Eventually, with practice and less self-imposed pressure, I enjoyed the process more and improved as a speaker.

When we give ourselves the gift of love even when we fall short of our aspirations, we have a better chance of achieving the results we desire and will enjoy the process much more. Remember that what you focus upon, you become.

* *Focus on the good in yourself, even when making mistakes. Knowing your behavior will help you do better the next time. In a notebook or journal, list five recent incidents and rank yourself from 1 to 10 (the highest being 10) for one or more of the following: loyalty, honesty, patience, friendliness, punctuality, organization, thoughtfulness, and creativity. Make this a weekly exercise to see your progress.*

* *Example: Received more change from the cashier than was owed and returned the excess. Honesty: 10, Patience: 10.*

* *Example: Yelled at my child for his or her messy room and later apologized. Patience: 2, Thoughtfulness: 2, Honesty: 8.*

A New Attitude

A few years ago, Kathy used to be one hundred pounds overweight. Then one day, as she was feeling self-hatred from looking at her thighs, "I had an idea that changed my life. I realized that my legs were precious. They carried me around and enabled me to do all that I do on a daily basis. Instead of hatred, I began to feel grateful." She replaced her berating attitude with one of appreciation, and as a result, went on to lose one hundred pounds.

When you accept yourself just as you are, then you can change.

Be Patient With Yourself

Wouldn't it be nice to go from where we are in our growth and development right to the mountaintop of spiritual mastery? In our microwave culture, we want things quick, fast, and in a hurry. Our desire for the instant fix carries over into our approach to and expectations of the spiritual path. We read one book after another, hoping to find a speedy, easy way to overcome all of our hang-ups and fears so we can live happily ever after. However, there aren't any quick fixes to our personal or spiritual growth. *We must mine the ore of Super You through patience and perseverance.*

Since we are not able to go from where we are to where we want to be spiritually in a single bound, it is vital that we be patient with ourselves. Spiritual growth is a long-term project. We never reach the point where the journey is over, even when the journey becomes easier, and eventually effortless. Instead of being impatient, make a commitment to knowing God, your Spiritual Self, for the long haul and to be patient along the path. Why not enjoy the process? After all, we are amazing creatures on an extraordinary journey.

A Lovable Soul

Harlan in his sixties had a military-style flattop haircut and wore Hawaiian t-shirts in the dead of a Missouri winter, smoked like a chimney, and was quite ornery at times. Despite his quirks or maybe because of them, Harlan was a lovable soul. Occasionally he said, "If you think I'm bad now, you should've seen me before I found spirituality."

Harlan made a good point.

* *Instead of looking at how far you are from the summit of spiritual perfection, take time to acknowledge how far you have come. Circle each of the following behaviors you have engaged in over the past six months:*

* *Cooked or bought a meal for a friend or family member*

* *Gave directions to a stranger*

* *Smiled at a stranger*

* *Gave a sincere compliment without an ulterior motive*

* *Provided a helping hand to someone in need*

* *Listened to a friend's problem or issue*

* *Prayed for yourself or someone else*

* *Read or listened to an inspirational work*

* *Cried during a touching scene in a movie*

* *Was helpful or constructive for another person*

* *Worked after hours to complete an important project*

* *Had empathy for a stranger*

Experience Your Emotions

Many of us were taught to fear our emotions. We grew up believing our feelings are unpredictable, irrational, and dangerous, and that we must keep them hidden. Because of these attitudes, many people are afraid of losing control and being overwhelmed by their feelings. They fear that if they let themselves feel their sadness, they will cry forever. They worry about hurting someone if they let themselves be angry. Also, there are others who are hesitant to acknowledge negative emotions because they fear that such emotions will attract negative circumstances.

Blocked emotions are a contributing factor to physical ailments. Burying emotions such as anger, resentment, and fear cause them to go underground, resulting in angry outbursts or physical illness. Pushing down emotions is like compacting trash. After a while, the trash begins to smell. If such emotions are within you, then you need to allow yourself to feel them in order to heal them. Otherwise, you will still carry around the feelings, which will attract negative circumstances. It's better to consciously feel those emotions so that you can heal and release them.

How can we accept our emotions? First, refrain from labeling emotions as good or bad. Think of your emotions as energy. You are not bad or unspiritual for having painful emotions. They are as much a part of the human condition as the so-called "good" emotions. Instead of labeling the emotion, let it be what it is, neither good nor bad.

Many of us believe that there are two doors in our consciousness. We want to close the door on our negative emotions and open the door to our positive ones. However, there is only one door through which all emotions must pass, both the pleasant and painful ones. To become Super You, it's important to experience the full range of emotions that come through our consciousness, a practice in Zen Buddhism called "walking the razor's edge."

What you discover in accepting your self is that emotions are like clouds in the sky. Soon, the clouds change and pass through. Very often when you become aware of what you are feeling *without resistance*, the emotion will begin to change. Rather than losing control when you are angry, the anger loses its power. Rather than crying forever when you feel sadness, you will cry just enough to experience a release of sorrow.

Rather than resisting what you are feeling, allow yourself to feel whatever is present and remember that you are not your emotions. You are a spiritual being who has emotions. Stand back and observe the emotions without getting caught up in them. Of course, you won't want to continue thinking the same thoughts that created the emotions in the first place, but allow yourself to feel whatever surfaces in your consciousness before switching your focus to create more pleasant emotions.

The following is a method for becoming aware of your emotions, which is an adaptation of a process taught by Robert Scheinfeld in his book, *Busting Loose from the Money Game.*

Once you allow yourself to feel the uncomfortable emotion, acknowledge that the emotion and the situation that triggered it are temporary and transitory. The emotion is not the reality of your Spiritual Self, which is an expression of love, joy, and power. Consciously withdraw the energy that you have invested in the negative thoughts and perceptions by saying to yourself, "I now withdraw my energy from _____ (the person, situation, or circumstance). Then say, "I feel the power flowing back into me now." Take a moment to feel it. Know the truth of your true identity as a spiritual being by saying to yourself, "I am God expressing itself as me. I am a powerful being of love, joy, and peace." Tell yourself the highest truth you know about your true self and the person or situation that triggered the uncomfortable emotions.

You don't have to use the exact words. But whenever you feel discomfort, take time to allow yourself to process the emotion, reclaim your power, and know the truth of your Spiritual Self. This can take a few moments or longer, depending on the intensity of the emotion and the time available to process it. You may need to apply this several times to the same situation and emotions in order to release the emotion and reclaim the power.

It is also important to have people in your life who see you as you truly are and accept you even when accepting yourself seems impossible. There are times when it is helpful to talk with a close friend or even a professionally trained person about what you are experiencing, which can help you to accept and release the hurtful emotions. Become one with the emotions or memories you dread by allowing yourself to experience them rather than covering them up with an overlay of positive thinking.

When you become aware of the emotions, they are transformed into a wellspring of joy and power.

Nurture Your Physical Self

Many people behave as if prayer and spiritual activities replace taking care of their physical bodies. However, our physical bodies are vehicles for Super You. The laws that govern our bodies are also part of God's laws.

In addition to spiritual activities, give your body the nutrition, exercise, and rest that it needs. In yoga philosophy, a spiritual aspirant will not access higher realms until the lower realm of the body is placed into a proper state of balance. The main purpose of yoga postures is to allow the body to sit still and pain-free during meditation, which is difficult to do in an unhealthy body.

Much is written in the West about nutrition and exercise. However, a subject that is not given a lot of emphasis in Western culture, and particularly in America, is the need for rest. Rest is often given low priority, especially in a country that was founded by pioneers and business innovators who worked tirelessly. As a result, we have a society where even the most underprivileged have the opportunity through hard work to flourish economically. This is certainly part of the American dream, but *we live in a society that has not been taught the value of rest.*

Our country's value system is that the busier we are and the longer hours we work, the more important we must be. Stress related symptoms are badges for how committed the person is to success in that company and chosen field. For every 90 to 120 minutes of energy that we expend, we should take a break to eat a healthy snack, stretch, breathe deeply, or do something that helps renew our mind and body. Then we are able to return to our work with greater enthusiasm and energy. Instead, what often happens is that we ignore our body's signals and gradually begin taxing our adrenal and nervous systems. Eventually, this leads to physical problems.

I love to achieve things, and have at times struggled with giving myself permission to rest and play. One Sunday afternoon I spent an hour parked in front of a video store, wrestling with whether I should rent a movie or go home and work. After that experience, I gave myself permission to watch a movie or do something else fun on Sunday afternoons. This helps me to be more cheerful and enthusiastic when needing to work, knowing that I have leisure time to look forward to. *Although I realize that my spiritual nature is joy and that I should not need something to look forward to in order to be happy, I throw my humanness a bone every now and then.* Many Sundays I have enjoyed a date with Ben & Jerry's and Netflix

An important part of being rested is getting enough sleep. Most Americans are sleep-deprived and need at least one to one-and-a-half more hours of sleep per night for maximum performance.

For years, I slept eight hours a night and felt too guilty to rest when I was sleepy during the day. Now I sometimes take a power nap in the afternoon, which lasts from ten to thirty minutes. I've been snickered at on more than one occasion for expressing an intention to take a nap, but afterwards I am renewed, refreshed, and re-energized until bedtime. Many business and political leaders have taken power naps, like Thomas Alva Edison, John F. Kennedy, and Sir Winston Churchill. It's important to listen to the wisdom of your body even when the mind disagrees. After all, your body is a vehicle for Super You.

Accept Your Sexuality

Years of social and religious conditioning have made sexuality a vexing subject in the context of spirituality. Sexual energy is one of the most powerful forces we deal with as human beings, and has been misunderstood and misused throughout history.

Many people are ashamed of their sexual desires, feeling that they are somehow bad or shameful for having them. These beliefs and resulting feelings have been passed down from Puritan times. We live in a strange society in which sex is exploited to sell almost everything, yet many people are ashamed of their sexual desires. There are also spiritual aspirants who believe that sexuality is animalistic and not spiritual, and they should be free from its promptings. Let's face it: sexual expression is one of our basic needs as human beings. *It's time we quit pretending that being spiritual means that we are above sexual feelings.* I have dated many spiritual women, and my experience has been that ninety-nine percent of them are not only spiritual but also hot blooded. I'm not complaining.

A mother and her eleven-year-old boy were watching a movie on television when a woman wearing shorts bent over. The boy said excitedly, "I sure do like that." Sex is in our blood. Men and women are attracted to one another, even from the earliest years. Young boys and girls vie for each other's attention.

When I studied spirituality in college, I was restrictive in my thinking about sex. Dad took me to Europe as a graduation gift and I walked out of the Moulin Rouge in Paris because looking at topless women was wrong and God didn't approve. Yet days later when swimming on the French Riviera, a beautiful woman popped out of the water like Bo Derek in the movie *10*. I didn't turn away in disgust but was excited by the appearance of this mermaid.

Acknowledge your sexual feelings and be aware of them when they surface. They are natural, not taboo. Because of this acceptance, sexual feelings do not control me. Though I enjoy looking at attractive women, my sexual nature is quiet. I am happy and content with or without.

You live in a physical body. Knowing your spiritual nature is not going to override millions of years of sexual evolution. People have sexual feelings until the day they die. If you don't believe me, watch an older man's eyes when an attractive woman walks by. Listen to an older woman's comments about how handsome a certain movie star is or her granddaughter's boyfriend. In a retirement community of 10,000 in South Carolina, rumors are rampant about the friskiness of the older folks. I'll spare you the details. So don't let the white hair fool you.

An important part of being human is accepting your sexual nature and not pretending that you're above animalistic thoughts or desires or even worse, try to hide from them and pretending they don't exist. Being real with yourself about your sexual thoughts and feelings not only makes you healthier, stronger, and more self-controlled, but also makes you a more interesting person.

Being spiritual and loving God doesn't change the fact that we have sexual feelings. Human beings seek pleasure, and some of the most pleasurable experiences come through sexual activity. Rather than being ashamed, feeling guilty, or pretending that we are not sexual beings, accept that you have sexual feelings and give appropriate expression to them. Repressing and pretending that you are too spiritual to have sexual feelings can backfire. Perhaps this accounts for the spiritual teachers who have fallen from grace because of their hidden sexual exploits or the many stories about cranky nuns in Catholic schools.

There are spiritual traditions that speak of sublimating sexual energy to contribute to higher states of consciousness and creativity. Sublimation does not mean repression, but rather a channeling of energy into other endeavors. Sublimation also does not mean complete abstinence, although this may be right for some. Each person's path is unique. One reason I lived at an ashram in Northern California was to find an answer to the question of whether I ought to be celibate. While there, I learned that this spiritual community started out with only monks and nuns living there. They soon discovered they liked each other too much. The community adapted when they realized that celibacy is not for everyone, and people must listen to their own nature. Now they have married couples, families as well as people who have chosen a life of celibacy. I came to grips with the fact that dating, not a lifelong vow of celibacy was my path and that it was okay. I also have learned that sexual feelings do not have to rule over you. The more aware and accepting you are of your humanness, including your sexuality, the more control you will have and be driven by your Spiritual Self, not your humanness.

Being Real With Others

Accepting all of yourself allows others to be who *they* are. The more you practice accepting others, the more you accept yourself. When you are vulnerable and share your humanness with someone you trust, it creates a closer connection. When they listen without trying to change you and still love you, you feel accepted on a deeper level. They will feel safer being real with you and sharing their own humanness.

Unveil Super You

As we accept our humanness, we peel back the layers that enclose our Spiritual Self. This is illustrated by the following story: In 1957, a group of monks in Thailand were moving their monastery. The monks had to move a ten-and-a-half-foot-tall clay Buddha that weighed over two-and-a-half tons. The Buddha cracked as it was being hoisted with a crane. Then it began to rain.

The head monk decided to lower the Buddha and cover it with a tarp. After a while, he looked under the tarp to see if the Buddha was being protected. When he looked at the crack, a gleam of light shone back at him. *With curiosity, the monk chiseled away at the clay. After hours of work, the monk found a solid gold Buddha, worth over a hundred million dollars.*

Historians believe that Thai monks hundreds of years earlier had covered the Buddha statue in clay to hide it from the invading Burmese army. The army killed all of the monks, and so it wasn't until years later that the golden Buddha was uncovered.

Like the gold Buddha, our spiritual potential is covered with the clay of our humanness. Through patiently acknowledging and embracing the layers of our humanness, we allow the gold of our Spiritual Self to shine through.

Step One Exercises

1. *Practice self-acceptance by looking in the mirror and saying: "I am enough," or "I like you," or "I love you." When you do something well, look in the mirror and say: "Thank you" or "You did great." When you make a mistake, go to the mirror and say: "I forgive you. Everyone makes mistakes. Next time, you'll do it differently."*

2. *Repeat to yourself, "I like myself" fifty times a day. This simple exercise can help you move through difficult experiences in which it would be easy to succumb to a victim mentality. By expressing loving thoughts to yourself, you open a way through which the love from your Spiritual Self within can be expressed.*

3. *Describe the last time your humanness prevailed. For example, eating a pint of Häagen-Dazs while on a diet. How did you feel about yourself? The next time you fail to live up to your spiritual ideal, pause and say, "I apologize. I like myself." Learn from the situation and decide to do it differently next time. Say, "I have not yet succeeded," which means that eventually you will succeed.*

4. *Describe a habit or behavior that has caused you difficulties. In a notebook or journal, write down your feelings as a result of this habit. Instead of indulging in self-critical thoughts, go for a full day observing the behavior without judging yourself or the behavior as bad. Don't try to change, just be aware. At the end of the day write what you experienced. Change follows once the habit or behavior is seen for what it is.*

5. *Be aware of your emotions for one day, all your emotions. Take a notebook or journal with you and write them down when they occur. Instead of labeling an emotion as good or bad, just be aware. Feel the emotions and write down what happens when you do. This is your humanness.*

6. *Practice the "Act As If" principle. If you're sad, whistle a cheerful tune and replace the sadness with joy. Think about the blessings in your life. Stand up straight and look at the sky more often. Consciously speak with a cheerful tone of voice. Force a smile until it comes naturally. Soon you will be joyful.*

7. *Wouldn't it be nice to live in a world where everyone feels good about who they are and spreads these feelings to others? Help a friend, spouse, or family member experience the transformation of self-acceptance by telling them they can download this chapter for free at www.superyoubook.com/bookbonus.*

Step Two

Relax and Release Super You

"Nature does not hurry,
yet everything is accomplished."
—Lao Tzu

At nine o'clock on Sunday morning, I left my fourth floor apartment at the Unity Center of New York City to the bookstore in the basement. I wanted to have a few books for sale that were related to my talk that morning in the eleven o'clock service at Lincoln Center's Avery Fisher Hall. I walked down to the basement, opened a door that closed behind me, and entered the small hallway leading to the bookstore. I tried to open the door to the bookstore. It was locked. I was trapped in a narrow hallway and no one else was in the building. I was scheduled to give the Sunday message in less than two hours, and there was no way out.

Hearing peoples' voices in the building next door, I started banging a code on the locked metal door that I had learned in camp as a boy. Three rapid knocks followed by three slow knocks followed by three rapid knocks stood for S.O.S. Since there was no response back, I figured no one else went to camp.

I did what any spirit-centered person would have done. I panicked. Well, actually I prayed. Trusting that I would be delivered, I re-worked my message for that morning, using the situation I was in as an illustration. Afterwards, I recited out loud the words of the author Emile Cady, "God is my deliverance. God is my deliverance," I paced up and down the hallway speaking these powerful words. With a burst of energy, I kicked the door handle and broke it. The alarm went off, not because of the door, but from an employee of the Center looking for me. Eventually he found me in the hallway. After opening the door, he reached up and removed a key that had been there the entire time. I had been too busy trying to come up with a solution instead of listening within where I might have heard, "Look above the door." That is how it often happens: we are so busy struggling that we forget to pause, relax, and let Spirit solve the problem through us. I arrived at Lincoln Center just in time to deliver my message, which was entitled, "Your Healing *Break*-through." (Listen to a free download of Justin's message by going to www.superyoubook.com/bookbonus.)

Many parts of our lives are centered in action. It seems like the world is speeding up; there are ever more things to do and places to be. In our modern world, action is highly valued, yet we often hear that people are stressed out or overworked, and spas and relaxation techniques have become very popular.

When we lose sight of our connection with Source and try to do everything by our own efforts, we are filled with tension and stress, and lose enjoyment of the process. Instead, *find a balance between doing your part and letting God be expressed through you. When you allow Spirit to express, or let it happen in your life, you can experience a greater sense of joy, because that is the very essence of who you are as a spiritual being.*

What is it that we are trying to do in our lives? In the final analysis, we are all looking for happiness. Aristotle said that all human motivation comes from this innate desire, and Pierre Teilhard de Chardin, the French paleontologist and Jesuit theologian, noted that, "Joy is the most infallible evidence of the presence of God."

Our world came into existence through a process of *letting*. "And God said: let there be light." (Genesis 1:3) The world was born, not through stress or strain, but through letting. The story of Adam and Eve in the Garden of Eden is symbolic for being in tune with Spirit. When they forgot their connection, then they had to earn their way through "in the sweat of thy face." (Genesis 3:19) When you lose sight of your connection with Source, then you try too hard and become filled with tension, stress, strain, and lose a sense of the joy and beauty of life. You need to find a balance between doing your part and letting God be expressed.

Fame and Fortune

Wally "Famous" Amos, the creator of the original Famous Amos chocolate chip cookies, discovered the power of letting things happen and experienced more joy early on in his career. He took a loan from friends and began in what he called a "small cubbyhole on Hollywood's Sunset Strip." Initially, Wally tried to force things to happen and became frustrated. He began his turnaround when he said to himself: "I don't want to be a big shot. I want to be happy." Wally let go of his tension and strain and let God do the work *through* him. His advice is to stop trying to make it happen, and instead let it happen.

When you let things happen, not only do you experience a greater sense of joy, but also get out of the way and your purpose begins to unfold. In this chapter, you will find how to let it happen more in your life.

Let God Solve Your Problems

You never need to feel alone when faced with a problem. When you acknowledge Spirit's presence in the middle of any trial, when you know with faith that your solution exists, it will arrive at the right and perfect time.

From Snow to Sun

Debi lived in Cleveland and her daughter lived in South Carolina. "It would be perfect, Mom, if you moved here," her daughter encouraged. Debi said, "When I retire, I will." She promised to visit every October for her daughter's birthday. The first year she did, she looked at homes. When she found one in a retirement community, she said, "Wow, this is it." However, she wasn't old enough for the community. But she took a model floor plan of one of the homes with her and said, "This is where I'm going to retire." She hung it on her refrigerator. Every October when Debi visited her daughter, she went back to that community and went through the model home with an inner knowledge that it was the right one for her. Three birthdays later, she found out that the community sold a certain number of houses to fifty year olds. Her immediate thought was, "If I build now, the house will be finished in April. I'll be fifty in August, so this might work out." She said to herself, "I can find a job, I'll do it." She signed the contract to go forward with building the home and returned to Cleveland. She gave her boss a six-month notice. He responded, "You're out of your mind. You don't have a job. You have a house to sell. What are you going to do? That's very irresponsible." Debi, however, felt that things had always worked out for her, and that they would again. Periodically, the boss would ask, "Did you find a job yet?" Deb's response was, "Yes. I just don't know where." "Did you sell the house yet?" "Yes, I just don't know to whom yet. It will happen perfectly."

This went on for six months. When she put her house on the market in 2007, her realtor told her that the market was on a downturn and she wasn't confident the house would sell. Debi continued to believe that the house would sell and acted as if things would work out perfectly, even hiring a person to replace her. During a massive blizzard in Cleveland, Debi received a call from an interested employer and two weeks later she had a job. One week later, she received an offer on her house that she accepted. One month later, she was living in her dream home in Hilton

Head, South Carolina near her daughter. Her advice is to "Let go and let God because God takes care of everything. All you have to do is put out there what you want, and it will show up at the right time."

The Golden Key

Author and lecturer Emmet Fox taught the practice of the Golden Key. Instead of thinking about your problems, think about God. Instead of filling your mind with anxiety, fear, worry, struggle, and strain, give your attention to Spirit and let your super potential be expressed.

Sometimes, we face a problem and don't know what to do. We are powerless as to the right way to go. As you might be aware, admitting you are powerless is the first of the twelve steps in Alcoholics Anonymous. You must admit your powerlessness over alcohol and acknowledge the presence of a Higher Power to heal and move on.

God, which encompasses the entire Universe, is wholeness. All the parts are working together in perfect timing and perfect order. No matter what the problem is, you can relax and let God, expressed as your Spiritual Self, solve it through you. As soon as you relax and trust, then you become receptive to creative ideas as well as the energy and wisdom to carry them out.

Surrender to Source

Jennifer was only fifteen years old when her mother died. To add to her distress, her father met and married another woman less than a year later. Jennifer's stepmother, Sheila, had tried very hard to make their new relationship comfortable. But whenever Sheila reached out, Jennifer exploded with rage and rebellion. Jennifer resented having a stepmother and sabotaged her father's marriage at every opportunity. The relationship between Jennifer and Sheila became intolerable to the point where Sheila considered divorce.

Sheila sought spiritual counseling, and learned to surrender her problems to spirit for the perfect resolution. She admitted being powerless in the relationship with her stepdaughter and allowed Source to work through her. As soon as she relinquished her power, she experienced a sense of transcendental peace.

When Jennifer came home from school the next day and started yelling at Sheila for doing her laundry without asking, Sheila relaxed and had faith that Spirit would show the way. For the first time, she saw the hurt little girl hidden in the angry teenager. She was prompted to go over to Jennifer and hug her. At first she was surprised, but Jennifer hugged back. They hung on to each other and started sobbing uncontrollably, and then they sat and talked for three hours.

Their relationship has been harmonious ever since, and Sheila credits it to her ability to surrender the relationship over to Source. She has perfect peace knowing she is not alone with her problems and that perfect solutions do exist.

Have a Sense of Humor

You can let it happen and release joy—which heals sorrow and gives you the capacity to cope—by tapping into your sense of humor, particularly in seemingly stressful situations.

President Ronald Reagan captured the heart of a nation after being shot in an assassination attempt, when he whispered, "I forgot to duck." We are inspired by people who choose a sense of humor in the face of trying circumstances because they remind us of the unique human ability to choose our response to what life hands us. Italian poet and philosopher Giacomo Leopardi said, "He who has the courage to laugh is almost as much a master of the world as he who is ready to die."

Not only does humor make any situation less dire, but it also releases the endorphins necessary to think and respond more effectively.

Oval Office Humor

Abraham Lincoln's cabinet members were assembled in the Oval Office. They were all long-faced and silent. Lincoln walked in, pulled a little book of humor from his pocket, and started to read. He read an entire chapter. Every now and then, Lincoln would pause and laugh.

In the meantime, his cabinet members grew irritated. They looked at each other, and mumbled, "What is he doing? This is sacrilegious, laughing at a time like this." But Lincoln kept reading and chuckling.

Finally, when he came to the end of a chapter, the

President took a big sigh and said, "Gentlemen, why aren't you laughing? Night and day I have such burdens and such stress that if I couldn't laugh I would die. And you need to laugh also." Then he took a piece of paper from his stovepipe hat and read the Emancipation Proclamation.

A sense of humor is something that we have because it is an innate aspect of our spiritual nature. Releasing this innate humor and joy gives us the capacity to cope with and triumph through life's challenges.

There are many people who believe that joy and humor have no place in religion. However, the meaning of the word religion means, "to bind together." True religion is realizing your oneness with God, the source of all joy and humor. A person who is living from his spiritual nature will naturally have a good sense of humor.

Many spiritual superheroes had a good sense of humor. Jesus told the story of the Prodigal Son, who squandered his inheritance on riotous living and ended up eating husks in a pigpen. Not a kosher situation for a young Jewish man. Many pictures of Jesus show him as a somber person, but my favorite and perhaps the most accurate depiction is of Jesus laughing. "These things have I spoken unto you, that my joy might remain in you, and that your joy might be full." (John 15:11)

Jesus also said, "Except ye be converted, and become as little children, ye shall not enter into the kingdom of heaven." (Matthew 18:3) One of the qualities of children is their ability to play. Many adults have lost the ability to play. We have become too sophisticated or too involved in projects and other peoples' lives and have forgotten to enjoy our own.

- *Your favorite childhood games are still with you, though they may be temporarily forgotten. Here are some ways to reclaim them and play as an adult.*

- *Enjoy the swings at a local park*

- *Play with your cat or dog*

- *Tell a joke or a funny story to a friend*

- *Dance to a favorite song at home*

- *Be silly with a friend*

- *Wear an outrageous hat or t-shirt*

- *Purchase a toy for yourself*

- *Blow soap bubbles*

- *Wear a fun tie or scarf*

- *Organize charades at the next office party*

Let yourself be silly once in a while. The word silly is derived from the Old English word *(ge) saelig*, which means to be blessed with happiness, prosperity, and health. Who wouldn't like that? Strive to be more childish and less adult-ish.

Charles Fillmore, the co-founder of the Unity Church, loved to tell funny stories. Paramahansa Yogananda played practical jokes. One evening while having dinner with his students, he pulled out a squirt gun and shot at the ceiling so that the water dripped down on the head of one of his best students. When Eric Butterworth was in the hospital after fracturing his hip, a visitor pointed to the intravenous bag and asked, "What are you eating?" Eric responded, "Ham and eggs." The more in touch we are with our Spiritual Self, the more we can put our life and the world in perspective and be happy in the middle of it.

How to Be a Nun

Saint Theresa of Avila looked for novices who, first of all, had a good appetite. Second, they had to be able to get a good night's sleep. And third, they had to laugh well. She believed that if they ate well, they were healthy. If they slept well, they did not have any big sins on their conscience. If they laughed well, they could handle life's difficulties.

"He that sitteth in the heavens shall laugh." (Psalms 2:4) This is not a reference to God sitting on a throne in the sky and laughing. Rather, sitting in the heavens refers to seeing life from a high perspective and looking on the bright side. No matter what is going on, you can tap into your spiritual potential and be able to cope.

In *Beyond Survival*, former POW Captain Gerald Coffee describes being ordered to wash himself in a rat-infested shower room littered with rotten bandages and garbage. Coffee was in deep despair. Lifting his head, he saw words by an American etched at eye level, "Smile, you're on Candid Camera." Coffee laughed aloud at the incongruity of the situation and had a deep appreciation for the man who in frustration, pain, and uncertainty could find it within himself to write those encouraging words. Coffee and others under similar circumstances were able to cope because they tapped into their sense of humor, that transcendent aspect of themselves, releasing inner strength and willpower, enabling them to meet the challenges they faced.

Recent medical research indicates that joy and laughter may alleviate allergy symptoms, increase pain tolerance, bolster the immune system, reduce the risk of stroke and heart attack, and help diabetics control their blood sugar.

Joy and laughter are innate aspects of our spiritual nature, and there are ways that you can stir up the joy and laughter within. Some say that it's impossible to think negative thoughts with a smile on your face. When you are in a bad mood and feel like anything but smiling, force yourself to smile and soon any gloomy thoughts and feelings are replaced with a more cheerful disposition.

* *Look in the mirror; put a big silly grin on your face for an entire minute. Do this five times a day for five days, and you will find a whole new spirit of joy developing within you.*

* *Another exercise is practiced by comedian Steve Martin: Stand in front of a mirror and make yourself laugh for two whole minutes. Your stress level will diminish and you will feel more light-hearted and joyful throughout the day.*

A very cheerful woman gave me the following words to a song that she learned in the third grade. The song is entitled, "You Can Smile."

> There are many troubles that will burst like bubbles,
> There are many shadows that will disappear;
> When you learn to meet them, with a smile to greet them,
> For a smile is better than a frown or tear.
>
> Though the world forsake you, joy will overtake you,
> Hope will soon awake you, if you smile today;
> Don't parade your sorrow, wait until tomorrow,
> For your joy and hope will drive the clouds away.
>
> When the clouds are raining, don't begin complaining,
> What the earth is gaining should not make you sad;
> Do not be a fretter, smiling is much better,
> And a smile will help to make the whole world glad.
>
> You can smile when you can't say a word,
> You can smile when you cannot be heard;
> You can smile when it's cloudy or fair,
> You can smile anytime, anywhere.

Take Yourself Lightly

It has been said, "Angels can fly because they take themselves lightly." We have a tendency to take ourselves too seriously because of an inflated sense of our importance and indispensability. Perhaps Plato was guilty of over-statement when he said, "No human thing is of serious importance."

In college, I took myself too seriously. In one instance, I was preparing a presentation for a communications class. I asked the professor about the practice of mirroring a person's behavior in order to establish rapport as being potentially manipulative. He said, "A knife can be dangerous depending on how it's used and the intentions of the person using it." At some point in the conversation he exclaimed, "Justin, you're not that important." The late Leo Buscaglia helped me take myself less seriously by explaining in his book, *Bus 9 to Paradise,* that the saints through the ages learned to laugh rather than cry about the suffering in the world. Joy does more good than sorrow for the healing of the world.

Jesus' disciples were incredulous when a woman started putting expensive oil on Jesus' feet when so many people in the world lacked the basic necessities. He said, "For the poor always ye have with you; but me ye have not always." (John 12:8) There will always be suffering in the world. In our times, it's easy to read or listen to the news and be overwhelmed by the wars, natural disasters, and poverty. However, being afraid and downcast does not make the world any better.

Yogananda encouraged people to be even-minded and cheerful at all times. Otherwise we lose perspective on life. Of course we also take practical steps to alleviate suffering and be empathetic. The point is to not sacrifice our own joy in the belief that doing so helps the world. It doesn't. Once I thought, "Being happy and content is the greatest difference I can make in the world." At that moment I heard a quiet voice within say, "You can't get any better." Mother Teresa, who spent her life serving the poorest of the poor, once reprimanded a nun saying that if she couldn't smile then she needed to find another vocation. In addition to food and medical care, the poor of Calcutta needed people who radiated a spirit of joy.

While we all have a unique and important mission to fulfill, it is erroneous, not to mention overwhelming, to think we are alone and separate in this endeavor. When you take yourself too seriously, you put forth the idea of your separateness from a greater power and block Spirit's expression through you, in order to help you. By taking yourself more lightly, you can get over your ego and thinking that you can bear the burdens of the world alone.

Humility at the Top

Abraham Lincoln sent a message to Edwin Stanton, his Secretary of War. When the messenger returned, Lincoln asked him what Stanton's response was. "He tore your letter up and said, 'Lincoln is a damned fool.'" Lincoln responded, "Then I dare say I must be one, for Stanton is generally right and he always says what he means."

Think of the embarrassing or difficult moments that happen to you as opportunities for a good story to tell. You might not able to laugh during the situation, or when it is fresh in your mind. Sometimes it takes years before you can look back and have a good chuckle over the incident. When you are going through something embarrassing, ask yourself how you'll feel about it in the distant future. You probably will have gotten over it and can find the episode amusing. Why wait when you can laugh about it now?

Years ago while working as an apprentice chef at a spiritual retreat located in the foothills of Northern California, my first assignment was to make soup, biscuits, and salad for thirty dinner guests. The problem was that I was also involved in yoga teacher training and had to demonstrate a yoga posture during the time I was supposed to be cooking. I started the meal, and then had a friend take over for me. I returned with forty-five minutes remaining before dinner was served. I tasted the soup and grimaced because there was way too much cayenne pepper. I quickly prepared drop biscuits but with only fifteen minutes remaining before dinner, the biscuits had failed to rise. A friend from yoga class observing me running around the kitchen offered to help. She tasted one of the questionable biscuits: "It looks and tastes like a cracker. Why don't you re-name them?" At this point, I was laughing and joyously running around the kitchen because of the ridiculousness of the situation and also trusting that Spirit would somehow work everything out. Fortunately, by the time dinner arrived, the cayenne had dissipated in the soup. After saying the blessing and announcing the soup, salad, and toppings, I unveiled the covered plate as "Virginia Flat Bread." People tasted them and said, "What do you call these? They're really good. Can I have the recipe?" An older man who also cooked for the retreat, whispered with a wry smile, "The biscuits didn't rise, did they?" I've always liked the saying, "He who knows how to laugh at himself will always have something to laugh about."

Keep a Positive Mindset

"For I know the thoughts that I think toward you, saith the Lord, thoughts of peace, and not of evil, to give you an expected end." (Jeremiah 29:11) Remember this in "letting it happen" by keeping a positive mindset. Your thoughts do not make things happen but allow the imprisoned splendor to be released from within.

Doing It Alone

"I am writing in response to your request concerning number eleven on the insurance form which asks for the 'cause of injuries' where in I put 'trying to do the job alone.' You said you needed more information so I trust the following will be sufficient.

I am a bricklayer by trade and on the date of injuries I was working alone laying brick around the top of a four-story building when I realized that I had about 500 pounds of brick left over. Rather than carry the bricks down by hand, I decided to put them into a barrel and lower them by a pulley that was fastened to the top of the building. I secured the end of the rope at ground level and went up to the top of the building and loaded the bricks into the barrel and flung the barrel out with the bricks in it. I then went down and untied the rope holding it securely to insure the slow descent of the barrel.

As you will note on number six of the insurance form, I weigh 145 pounds. Due to my shock at being jerked off the ground so swiftly, I lost my presence of mind and forgot to let go of the rope. Between the second and third floors, I met the barrel coming down. This accounts for the bruises and laceration on my upper body. Regaining my presence of mind, again I held tightly to the rope and proceeded rapidly up the side of the building, not stopping until my right hand was jammed in the pulley. This accounts for my broken thumb.

Despite the pain, I retained my presence of mind and held tightly to the rope. At approximately the same time, however, the barrel of bricks hit the ground and the bottom fell out of the barrel. Devoid of the weight of the bricks, the barrel now weighed about fifty pounds. I again refer you to number six of the insurance form and my weight.

As you would guess, I began a rapid descent. In the vicinity of the second floor I met the barrel coming up. This explains the injuries to my legs and lower back. Slowed only slightly, I continued my descent, landing on the pile of bricks. Fortunately, my back was only sprained and the internal injuries were only minimal. I'm sorry to report, however, that at this point I again lost my presence of mind and let go of the rope. As you can imagine, the empty barrel crashed down on me.

I trust this answers your concern. Please know that I am finished 'trying to do the job alone.'"

It is important to align your human self with your Spiritual Self and be willing to allow Spirit to express through you rather than trying to make things happen on your own. Source, who is present everywhere, wants to more fully express from within you into the world. However, **negative thoughts and beliefs unnecessarily block the natural expression of Spirit into our life and affairs.**

Negative thoughts weaken your immune system, making you more vulnerable to physical ailments. According to the American Institute of Stress, between seventy-five and ninety percent of all visits to primary care doctors are the result of stress. Habits of worry, fear, anger, hatred, and jealousy can weaken the immune system, inhibiting the flow of life force in the body, resulting in physical illness.

Saint Paul said: "…whatsoever things are true, whatsoever things are honest, whatsoever things are just, whatsoever things are pure, whatsoever things are lovely, whatsoever things are of good report; if there be any virtue, and if there be any praise, think on these things." (Philippians 4:8) Instead of filling your mind with negative thoughts, focus on the good in your life.

* *When you keep your thoughts on the good, then you allow the Kingdom of God that is within to unfold into outer experience. Answer the following questions to discover the good in your life:*

* *What gives you joyousness right now?*
   Your home
   Your children
   Your grandchildren
   A joke or funny story you recently heard
   A new project you are involved in
   A new movie

* *What are you grateful for?*
   Good health
   Sound mind

Loving partner or spouse
Stranger's kindness
Honest friend
Spiritual community
Your gifts and talents
Prayer and meditation

✱ *Since Spirit is wholeness and everything works together in perfect timing and order, expect the best to happen and maintain a positive attitude even in the face of setbacks and disappointments.*

The Right Balance of Doing and Letting

Paramhansa Yogananda calls a "superman" that person who is able to balance material and spiritual consciousness, or "doing" and "letting." There is a right balance between doing our part and letting Spirit express. Do your best and leave the rest. ***The result is a sense of inner freedom.***

People throughout the ages have searched for the balance between what is their responsibility and what belongs to God. Ancient people believed that Spirit was supposed to do everything and therefore, they did very little. The Buddha, in order to counter the passivity he witnessed, taught people they must do everything, emphasizing personal responsibility. Many of Buddha's followers believe that he was an atheist because he didn't talk about God. According to Paramhansa Yogananda, Buddha did not talk about God because his mission was to emphasize the need for the individual to make a spiritual effort rather than merely performing ceremonies and waiting passively for divine blessings.

Jesus taught the balance of personal responsibility with faith and activity. He said, "My Father worketh hitherto, and I work." (John 5:17) In modern parlance this means, "God helps those who help themselves."

In an urban area, a man had cultivated a small patch of land. A woman was out taking a stroll and on noticing the garden she said, "What a beautiful garden God has created." Shovel in hand, the man responded, "You should've seen it when God tended it alone."

Of course we can go to the other extreme, doing our part but then getting in our way by not letting go enough to allow Spirit to express.

Sometimes a person may think he or she is responsible for the healing of another. While we may be instruments through which Spirit expresses, God is really the healer. Silent Unity, the twenty-four-hour prayer service at Unity Village in Kansas City, Missouri, holds prayer meetings daily and opens them with the affirmation: "It is not I, but the Christ within, who does the work." Those at the meetings remember the truth that through their prayer efforts, they become avenues through which Spirit within does the healing work. We are instruments through which healing power, guiding wisdom, and prospering substance flow.

Divine Indifference

Eric Butterworth spoke about the time when he experimented with a biofeedback machine. This machine monitors involuntary functions of the body such as the heart rate. The biofeedback mechanism helps people learn how to consciously control blood pressure and other functions.

When Eric was hooked up to the machine, he was told that the objective was to make the needle on the machine rise. Eric thought, "This will be easy. After all, I am a metaphysician and have control over my thoughts." Through the power of his thoughts, he tried to make the needle go up, and alas, the needle went down. After a few failed attempts, he decided to take a different approach. Instead of trying hard to make the needle rise, he visualized it rising and became totally indifferent as to whether it did or not. And the needle rose.

Eric instructs, "If there is something that you desire to do, see it happening with a feeling of what I call 'Divine Indifference,' and it will happen. Don't pressure it, don't say, 'I want this to happen.' See it, get the vision of it, but then get the sense of 'it really doesn't matter' and you will begin to see the manifestation come forward in your life. 'Take no thought what ye shall eat and what ye shall drink and wherewithal ye shall be clothed,' said Jesus… no effort, no will, not to do but to let be done, to let God be God in you."

After meditation each morning, I spend time visualizing what I want to see happen in my life. At the end of the visualization, I surrender the results and the timing of them to Source. Of course, surrendering results and having an indifferent attitude toward them requires patience and persistence. *A Course in Miracles* says, "Infinite patience produces immediate results." The immediate results are inner peace, freedom, and joy. The manifestation occurs at the right and perfect time and in the right and perfect way. Of course, in addition to meditating and visualizing, we have to also move our feet.

Years ago when serving as an associate to Eric Butterworth, I faced the challenge of preparing Sunday messages and weekly seminars. At times, I found myself anxiously trying to finish them on time. A turning point came when I decided that having peace of mind and trusting God working through me was more important than the actual results. Repeating the affirmation "Divine intelligence is working through me now" helped me let go of worry, to trust and to enjoy the process more. As a result, the messages were done sooner and better.

Now when I prepare a message, I do my very best and trust that Spirit is doing the work through me. If I have a class at seven o'clock, I set a time, say five o'clock, at which point I put away my work and know that whatever is done is done. I take on a feeling of "divine indifference" about the results. I sometimes say aloud, "I don't care at all what happens or how it works out. God is the Doer." Then I enthusiastically look forward to what Source will say and do through me. When I trust the process, I am pleasantly surprised.

William James, considered the father of American psychology, cited many examples of people who had tried unsuccessfully for years to overcome anxieties, worries, inferiorities, and guilt feelings. It was only when they relaxed and gave up the feeling of responsibility, and became genuinely indifferent, that they released a greater power from within.

* *We should do the best we can, but with the awareness that we are letting God do it through us. Give thanks for your failures because through recognition of God, failure can result in a higher good and blessing. In a notebook or journal, list five failures in your life that turned out to be blessings.*

* *Example: One year after Eric Butterworth passed away, I left New York City and moved to Hilton Head Island, South Carolina where I became the senior minister of the Unity Center there.*

Ultimately, God does everything through us and as us. When you have this awareness, then you are free of the fear of failure. Also, do your very best not for the sake of impressing others or for the outer rewards alone but because of the satisfaction and joy of being an instrument through which Spirit expresses.

Swami Satchidananda said it well: "Somebody is doing everything through you. You have nothing to worry about, even if you make a mistake. Suppose you do your best and you still make a mistake. Then you made a mistake. If you think, 'I didn't do my best; somebody else did that best through me, and somebody else made the mistake,' then you are not responsible for doing the best or doing the worst. Literally speaking, none of us is doing anything here. There's only one doer: the Cosmic Intelligence that does everything and works through everybody." At the times when I fully embrace this teaching, I feel inwardly free and enjoy the process.

A very successful salesperson, author, and television personality for the past forty years said that throughout her life, she has felt a lot of fear and stress. She said that her desire is to not only be successful but to enjoy the journey.

Timothy Gallwey, author of the *Inner Game* series, explains that every activity consists of three components: performance, learning, and enjoyment. When a person focuses exclusively on performance, then performance declines. On the other hand, when he or she focuses on learning and enjoyment, performance improves. Focus more on consciously enjoying whatever you are engaged in and trust that the results will take care of themselves. Not only will you have more fun but also find that the results are better.

We could all benefit from the philosophy of Kenya's Olympic championship running team: "Run every day from youth on. And run so you will enjoy it the next day. Everything else will follow automatically."

Let Go For Your Loved Ones

No child is perfect and some are temporarily lost to the modern day temptations of substance abuse and crime. There is a method to free parents from worry and heartache, and more effective than trying to convince their children to change unhealthy behavior. Behold the presence of Spirit within your loved ones and trust that Spirit is there, even though appearances may say otherwise. Parents should know this for their children and trust that it is so. God works through them in the right and perfect time and way. They are the responsibility of God first and foremost.

If your children are adults, you did your best. Let them grow up and let Spirit grow them. Though adult children may bask in the attention and accept the continuous help, they often have unconscious resentment. They resent being treated as if they can't take care of themselves. When you affirm that Spirit is in them, you are affirming their potential and they have what it takes to succeed. Quiet confidence influences them on a deep, subconscious level. They feel it. More importantly, you become a vehicle through which Spirit can express through them.

Here is an affirmation from Emily Cady's *Lessons in Truth*: "The Holy Spirit lives within you. He cares for you and is working in you to will and to do whatsoever He wishes you to do and is manifesting Himself through you." I've used this for years and gained a lot of inner peace. Instead of agonizing over loved ones, know the truth for them. Listen to your inner guidance and take the action you are guided to take. Do your part and let Spirit come through.

Have the Spirit of Service

Some spiritual teachings say that even **more important than what you do is the spirit with which you do it**. Doing everything with a sense of joy brings greater benefit in the end in some mysterious way. When you act with a spirit of service, joy is a natural result.

Jesus said: "Give, and it shall be given unto you." (Luke 6:38) He taught that the more we give in life, the more we receive *from* life. It is the nature of Spirit to give and the Universe is ever-seeking to unfold more of itself through us and into the world. You can let your Spiritual Self unfold when you have the spirit of service.

In a lecture to people in the healing professions, Dr. Rachel

Naomi Remen, an early pioneer in mind-body medicine, explained the difference between "helping and fixing people" and "having the spirit of service." When we are helping and fixing others, we are in a consciousness of superiority and separation that says: "I am whole and the person I'm helping or fixing is not." However, when we are in the spirit of service, our attitude is: "I am a whole person through whom the Spirit expresses to bless another whole person." In the spirit of service, we tune into an unlimited flow of energy and joy.

Work and Service

Paramahansa Yogananda told his student, Mrs. Vera Brown: "You work too hard. You must work less. If you don't, you will ruin your health." She decided to take his advice and tried to work less. To her surprise, two or three days later, Yogananda gave her more work to do. She trusted he knew what he was doing, but wondered how she was going to follow his instruction when he was giving her extra work. A few days later, he again sternly told her: "You must not work so hard. In this lifetime you've done enough work for several incarnations." Again, she tried cutting down her activities only to have him give her more to do. This happened several times. Every time he told her to work less, he increased her duties. Finally, one day she looked at him and said: "Sir, instead of our using the word 'work' in our life here, why don't we substitute the word 'service'?" Yogananda laughed: "It has been a good show. All your life you've been thinking, Work! Work! Work! That very thought was exhausting you. But see how differently you feel when you think of work as a divine service."

Many spiritual traditions emphasize the importance of service. What would happen if you looked at your efforts in your career as service instead of work? Perhaps you would experience a greater sense of meaning and an increase in energy. Think of service as letting Spirit create and express *through* you.

According to Swami Satchidananda, the key to peace is to do everything with a spirit of service. Asking, "How may I serve?" removes the ego, our source of anxiety, fear, and suffering. When you are concerned about me, my, and mine, you fear not getting what you want and react with anger if your desires are thwarted. Joy and fulfillment well up from within when you focus on giving and serving out of love for God and people. And good shows up in your life.

I heard the still, small voice say to me in meditation, "Your satisfaction is in helping others." Having a spirit of service gives you a greater sense of meaning and an increase in energy. You begin attracting positive results but are detached from the outcome because your actions are for Spirit and for others. Outer success is a by-product. Service is letting God create and express through you, trusting that Spirit's will is the highest happiness and good for you and everyone involved.

✳ *We can do more with more joy when we have the spirit of service and let God express in us and as us. We please others and our self when we listen to and allow our Spiritual Self to be expressed. Next to each item in the list below, write the letter W for work or S for service.*

✳ *Wait tables in a restaurant*

✳ *Give an inspirational talk*

✳ *Computer consulting*

✳ *Sell a product or service*

✳ *Counseling*

✳ *Healing therapy*

✳ *Yoga*

✳ *Meditation*

✳ *Baking cookies*

✳ *Babysitting*

✳ *Homework*

✳ *Teaching*

✳ *Playing golf*

✳ *All the above activities can be service when done with a spirit of joy, helpfulness, and letting Spirit express. The Zen tale says, "Before enlightenment, chop wood and carry water. After enlightenment, chop wood and carry water." Your current work may not be what God is preparing you for, but done in the spirit of service it is a stepping-stone to your right place.*

See the Beauty in Life

In his book, *Body, Mind, and Sport*, John Douillard tells the following story: An English naval officer was marooned on a remote island in the South Pacific. He befriended a local villager to whom he was constantly trying to prove his own superiority and that of his culture. For the Englishman, everything was a contest, from who could build a better fire to who could design a more functional hut. This puzzled the villager because life to him was fun, like a game. He didn't understand the Englishman's competitive intensity.

One day, the Englishman challenged the villager: "We will have a race from here to that distant point." The villager agreed. The Englishman began to set up the conditions: "We will train in our own style, privately, for two weeks. On the fourteenth day, we will compete."

When the day arrived, they took their places on the starting line, and the Englishman fired his pistol in the air to set them off. With his usual intensity, pushing himself to the limit of his physical ability and grimacing with strain, the Brit drove himself through the sand and lunged for the finish line. Exhausted and soaked in sweat, he turned to see how his opponent was doing.

To his joy and amazement, the villager was only about halfway to the finish line. The Englishman watched him float gracefully along the shoreline with long, comfortable strides, a smile on his handsome face. When the villager finally pranced across the finish line, he found the

Englishman jumping up and down wildly: "I won, I won."

The villager looked at the Englishman in disbelief: "What? You won? No, I won. I was the most beautiful."

Let us, like the villager, "be the most beautiful." Stop the strain, worry, and struggle to win the race of life. Instead, enjoy the journey of letting it happen.

Step Two Exercises

1. *Think of a situation you are worried about or have difficulty overcoming. Consider the possibility that a solution exists. In a notebook or journal, write down the situation in detail; identifying the problem is fifty percent of finding the solution. Now get still and connect with your Spiritual Self. Write possible solutions on a separate page. See if one stands out from the others. If so, list the steps you can take to carry out the solution. If a solution does not stand out, trust that Source will continue to guide you and give you the solution at the right time. Use this affirmation, "I let go of tension, stress and strain, and I let it happen, with joy." Let the solution happen.*

2. *Choose an activity where you have a tendency to take yourself too seriously. In a notebook or journal, list ways you can enjoy yourself more while engaging in the activity, like playing relaxing music in the background. Refer to this list whenever you are stuck. Enjoying the process yields better performance in the long run.*

Step Three

Super Guidance

*"Something within me tells me
what I must do every day."*
—Albert Einstein

One Christmas over twenty years ago, I purchased gifts based on guidance I received during meditation. In one instance, my girlfriend's father, a six-foot-four burly fireman, opened his gift and exclaimed, "Ratchets. How did you know I needed these?" Then I unwittingly told him, "God told me." Eyebrows raised, he looked at his wife, "Mildred, God told him." The next month during my birthday celebration, I again acted upon an idea that surfaced during meditation and handed out roses to each person while the song, "The Rose," played in the background. The big guy got one also. My mother looks back on that day fondly. I look back wondering, "What was I thinking?"

My stepfather, Henry, now 85, recently told me, "Justin, you're tough. I wish I had done all of the things you have done." When you seek Spirit's guidance, you will do amazing things that you never dreamed of doing.

Paramhansa Yogananda wasn't always certain of Spirit's guidance and sometimes tested it. My friend Jim Rosemergy once heard Spirit say in meditation, "I am mystery. Unless mystery is a part of your life, I am not a part of your life." We are required to trust that God is guiding us at all times, even if we don't understand it ourselves.

In spite of having no conscious memory of where we as humans emerged from, we live and move in the flow of spiritual intelligence and wisdom.

While at times life may seem chaotic and random, undeniable evidence of perfection abounds. Everything seems to magically come together. Daytime turns into night, and back into daytime every single day; trees lose their leaves in the fall and gain them back in the spring; salmon swim thousands of miles upstream, returning to where they hatched to spawn.

We have been created with a navigation system that we can tap into to experience the expression of great and extraordinary good in our life. Because we don't know all of the answers from the level of ordinary consciousness, we need guidance each and every day. We can find those answers by tapping into the wisdom of our Spiritual Self.

The Spiritual Self can give you knowledge and guidance not readily perceivable with your five senses.

Finding Your Inner Guidance

Right now, answers to your questions and solutions to your problems exist within you. In fact, even before we know we have a problem, the answer is within us.

Many people lack confidence in the possibility of receiving spiritual guidance. They believe God is apart from them, residing far away in the sky, or only in church and other holy places. They believe that the Universe arbitrarily bestows wisdom on some people and withholds it from others. When they pray for guidance, they are uncertain whether they will receive it.

Spirit is omnipresent, and so are wisdom and intelligence. We do not need to convince God of anything or wonder whether we will be guided. Spirit *is* and so is wisdom. Wisdom is available, and our job is to accept and synchronize with it.

In Nature, We Call It "Instinct"

There is a guiding intelligence throughout nature, where it operates without self-consciousness. We call this instinct.

Chimpanzees in Tanzania's Gombe National Park will depart from their regular diet and eat rough, sharp, pungent leaves from a plant called aspilia. Local herbalists use the leaves for stomach upsets; they contain chemicals that attack harmful bacteria and stomach parasites.

For similar purposes, generations of elephants have risked their lives to visit a cave on the side of Mount Elgon, an extinct volcano in western Kenya. The elephants dig out the soft rock with their tusks, grind it with their teeth, and swallow it. The rocks contain a hundred times more sodium than the elephants can get from the plants they normally eat, and rich in potassium and calcium.

The same spiritual intelligence guides the arctic tern to fly as much as twenty thousand miles per year, from the Arctic to the Antarctic and back.

Like animals, humans use instinct for preserving the self and the species. However, we have even more than our instinct as guidance. We have intuition. Intuition is more personal, a spiritual intelligence that has different answers and wisdom for each of us, depending on our mission in this world and what we need for personal growth. Intuition is the internal spiritual guidance system that wants the best for us. You will recognize intuitive guidance as a strong hunch, gut feeling, or certain "knowing."

Be Willing and Fearless

The first step in following this amazing navigation system is to be willing to believe that it is available to you. Yes, it is available now by the fact that you are alive. Spiritual guidance is your birthright.

* *When you tap into your internal wisdom and receive guidance in whatever form, find small ways to follow it. This guidance really works, and your courage to follow will increase.*

* *You are about to leave home and feel you have forgotten something. Take a moment to think what that might be.*

✳ *You think about calling a friend you haven't spoken with in a long time. Call them and see what unfolds.*

✳ *You have an urge for a particular vegetable or other healthy product in the grocery store. Go ahead and buy it. Your body may be craving a vitamin or mineral from that particular food.*

✳ *You are drawn to read a particular book. Flip through the pages until your fingers stop. The passage or chapter may be what you need.*

✳ *Choose among a variety of movies by consulting your gut about which one feels right. An uneasy feeling about a movie means to choose another.*

✳ *If you wake from sleep earlier than normal, get up and begin your day. You might need more time to accomplish or participate in a certain activity.*

✳ *Listen to your gut feeling about a person when meeting them for the first time because often first impressions later prove to be accurate.*

Do not fear making wrong choices in following your spiritual guidance. While your choices may not always take you where you expect to go, attunement with your internal wisdom insures that you will learn from whatever choice you make, and grow in consciousness as a result. Should similar circumstances arise again in the future, make new and different choices that reflect your new consciousness. As we follow Spirit's guidance to the best of our ability, we can trust the promise that everything is working together for good to those who love God.

Being overly concerned, worrying, and fretting over what to do may prevent you from being in tune with the wisdom of your Spiritual Self. Ask yourself, "What would I do if I were not afraid?" This will give you some clarification about what you need to do.

The willingness to follow your spiritual guidance will magnify your ability to tap into it. "Ask, and it shall be given you; seek, and ye shall find; knock, and it shall be opened unto you." (Matthew 7:7)

I've made major decisions that have worked out merely because of my *sincerity* and *willingness* to follow spiritual guidance. When you are willing and sincere, you do not fear making a wrong decision; whatever decision you make will turn out for the best.

What's Trying to Happen Here?

Be aware of what God seeks to unfold in a situation. Ask the question "What's trying to happen here?" to get you out of trying to make things happen from your limited personal self, and be open to your inner guidance.

I was once in the middle of a church conflict. Both sides were unhappy with how the election for board members had been handled. The person who had won was under pressure from the losing side and elected into a difficult role. He told me months later that the advice to see "what's trying to happen here" enabled him to put aside what he wanted personally or thought *should* happen. Instead, he became open to the perfect solution. The result is that he listened empathically in a difficult situation, and the church discovered a solution that worked for everyone.

One way to tap into your internal wisdom is to put aside personal desires and be willing to do whatever is for the highest and best of all concerned. Get still, and become neutral and open. Be willing to go in any direction. When you have sufficiently turned your will over to your internal wisdom, you become more receptive to the light emanating from within.

The Best Option

The Unity Church on Hilton Head Island had a big question. Two months previously a new banquet hall opened in a hotel on the mainland. For years the congregation had talked about moving to the mainland to reach more people. They reserved the banquet hall and had to make a decision because another church wanted to rent the space. Churches are usually advised not to move more than seven miles from their present location because they could lose a significant number of members and go bust. The Unity Church considered moving fourteen miles away, and their biggest financial contributors lived on the island.

The congregation had four options, three of which involved doing one service on the island and one on the mainland. Doing two services in different locations required enormous volunteer support and organization. One morning during meditation, the minister had the impression of church members holding hands and meeting only on the mainland. He didn't mention this to anyone. During a meeting to discuss the options, an unexpected fifth option emerged, voiced by island and mainland people, the same that came to the minister in meditation. The Church moved to the mainland and attendance increased by fifty percent. By being sincerely open to what's trying to happen, Spirit

> revealed the best option, and they made the transition in a harmonious way. Eric Butterworth always taught, "You don't have to 'make' a decision. Let the decision 'make' you." Do not fear making a wrong choice in following your guidance.

Follow Your Enthusiasm

When you are neutral and open to whatever your internal wisdom is revealing you may have enthusiasm in one particular direction. This is a sign from your internal guidance system. Source is energizing and motivating you in the direction for your highest joy and fulfillment.

Enthusiasm comes from "en" and "theos," together meaning "in God." The Apostle Paul writes: "For it is God which worketh in you both to will and to do of his good pleasure." (Philippians 2:13) *Work* is from the Greek "energeo," which means energy. In essence, Paul says that Spirit is energizing and motivating you in the direction that is for your highest joy and fulfillment. When you feel genuine enthusiasm compelling you toward an action, it is often Source working in your heart, energizing and motivating you.

Following your joy and enthusiasm will guide you to the career choices directly in line with your unique life mission. Ask yourself, "What do I love doing? What am I good at? Does what I enjoy doing and do well fulfill a need that people would be willing to pay for?"

Within the answers to these questions lie clues. I once accepted a job as a telemarketer for a friend who sold herbal remedies. On the first day, I had no enthusiasm and felt an inner knowledge that it wasn't what I was supposed to be doing. My friend was grateful that I knew the job wasn't right for me before going through the training program. By not pursuing that job, the way opened up for another one for which I did have joy and enthusiasm.

You may have feelings of joy and a sense of the rightness of a particular option you are considering. Whenever I've had a lasting feeling of enthusiasm, joy, aliveness, and a sense of rightness about making some kind of change, it has always been for the best.

Sometimes you need to trust your inner enthusiasm for days, weeks, months, or years to fulfill what your internal wisdom is energizing you to do. Even when things are difficult, the enthusiasm within you will lead you where you should go. However, *when you don't follow your inner guidance, your energy can be blocked and deadened.* You may experience depression, numbness, or loss of energy or power. Repressing or ignoring your guidance can lead to illness, because you are blocking the inner flow of life.

Contentment and Guidance

I often wondered how contentment, desires, dreams, and goals and God's will all work together. My concern was that if I were content in the moment, I might miss where I ought to be. This discounts the omnipresence and the omnipotence of Spirit. When you are willing and trusting, God can guide you. However, you make it difficult for Spirit when you are anxious and restless. Life is a manifestation of your dominant thoughts, and discontent produces more of the same in the future. When you are content in the now, you become a clearer vehicle through which Source can express and guide you. After all, peace and contentment are expressions of Spirit. Since God's ultimate will is for you to know and express Spirit, contentment should be your primary goal.

Focus on being content by keeping your mind on God (see step four, "Living in the Super Zone," and step five, "Your Secret Hideout"). When you are content, desires will well up within you regarding how Spirit wants to express through you. When you are willing and happy in the now, the emerging urges and desires are from Source. And if they are not, the Universe will show you.

Always seek to be content and enjoy the journey. After all, you are God expressing as you. Spirit is happy and content in the eternal now. You are an eternal being and have forever to express your Self. When you make a decision, ask, "Would this lead to my own enlightenment?" When doing something for others, ask, "Would this contribute to her or his enlightenment?"

Take Action

God can't steer a parked car. It's better to do something than to sit around waiting for guidance.

* * *If you do not receive clear guidance, you can still take action. Frequently, guidance will clarify itself. Here are a few actions to consider:*

* * *Request a ten-minute information interview with someone in the career you are considering.*

❋ *Take an adult education class in your interests: stand-up comedy, art, music, or computers.*

❋ *Go to job interviews.*

❋ *Visit the area you want to move to.*

❋ *Make a coffee date with the man or woman you are interested in.*

Remember, guidance is available right now. If you're uncertain, do what makes the most sense and appears to be the best course of action. Act on the wisdom you have at the moment and understand that what you should do will become clearer in the process. When you are not going in the direction that is for the highest good of everyone concerned, it will become clear to you.

A Message for St. Francis

St. Francis of Assisi received a flash of guidance while praying in the ruins of a small chapel. He heard the message: "Rebuild my church." He looked at the ruins and assumed he was meant to reconstruct the chapel. He began to do so. As St. Francis acted on the guidance as he *understood* it, he recognized a deeper significance in the words; he was called to rebuild the entire Christian church. In taking a little bit of action, he became attuned to what Spirit was really directing him to do.

You may not receive a vision as St. Francis did or hear voices like Joan of Arc. However, when you do what makes the best sense in the moment, then you will be guided. If you are not going in the direction that is for your highest good and everyone concerned, it will be clear. Guidance frequently becomes clear when you move in a direction.

Tap Into Your Spiritual Wisdom Every Day

Your guidance can be in a certain direction for a while, but that can change. This is why you need to take time each day to check in with your Spiritual Self.

Jim had a telescope in his backyard. One night he went outside to look through it, but the sky was cloudy and he wasn't able to see the particular galaxies and star clusters he hoped to see. However, the experience was a good reminder of the fact that all of those stars and galaxies—even when he couldn't see them—were still present. The same is true with our inner guidance. You always have access to wisdom if you quiet the clouds of mental restlessness; this enables the light from Spirit to shine brightly in your consciousness.

Life is change, and we do not continue in the same direction forever. Security in the known is false security. Instead, find security in following your spiritual guidance, knowing that everything is working together for your highest good and that of others.

Wisdom of the Dream

Psychologist Carl Jung taught that tremendous insight about one's self can be gained by paying attention to the wisdom in a dream. During sleep, our conscious mind shuts down and we can become more receptive to guidance that is coming from a higher source.

Before going to bed, ask Spirit for an answer to a seemingly unsolvable problem. Either in a dream or on waking in the morning, you may have received an answer that can lead you in expansive and unexpected directions. I have done this many times and often didn't receive a clear answer. I've learned to ask and not worry about whether it is answered. Occasionally I receive some kind of guidance while sleeping, like a title for a Sunday message or ideas for a seminar. They come in their own timing.

Nineteenth-century author Robert Louis Stevenson claimed that he received the plots of his books mostly through his dreams.

Meeting Don

In his autobiography, *The Voices in My Head,* the late Danny Gans recounts how he finally got his big break to play professional baseball. That same afternoon, he was severely injured in practice, putting him in the hospital for a week with his right leg in a full-length cast. Sharing the hospital room with Danny was a man named Don Top, who had cancer and was scheduled for an operation to amputate his leg. Don was very talkative and wanted to know Danny's history. While Danny recounted a life full of accidents and misfortune, Don was overjoyed. At one point Danny asked what he was smiling about. "I'm scheduled for surgery tomorrow," he explained. "Worst case scenario is that I could get my leg cut off. But now I know that I'm not going to have to go through any of that...I'm here because of you. I'm your messenger. I've been sent here to tell you that God has another plan for your life that doesn't include baseball. God used baseball, for whatever reason, to bring you to this point in your life emotionally, physically, and spiritually to prepare you for what's next. But I have no idea what that is...do you?"

Minutes later, Don insisted that the surgeon only do an exploratory surgery on his leg and go no further. Soon the medical staff began entering and leaving his room. Some of the doctors stood around shaking their heads. The cancer they had found in their preliminary surgery was gone. They had no explanation. Danny kept in touch with Don for the next twenty years. Danny went on to become Entertainer of the Year in Los Vegas.

Confer with Wise Men and Women

When you face a decision that has big consequences at stake, talk with a person who has your best interests at heart and who is spiritually centered. "Where no counsel is, the people fall: but in the multitude of counselors there is safety." (Proverbs 11:14)

It may be best not to consult someone who has a vested interest in what you do, such as a best friend or family member, especially if he or she is not spiritually centered and able to be objective. Rather, talk with someone who is intuitive and impartial, such as a therapist, spiritual leader, or a friend who you know can be neutral.

When one or more people I consider intuitive and spiritually centered encourage me to go in a certain direction, it is usually the right path to take. Still, regardless of support from others or criticism, you ultimately must accept responsibility for the decision. What you decide to do must feel right to *you*.

Recognize Your Own Wisdom

Many of us constantly look over our shoulder, hoping to please our father, mother, or spouse or to live up to cultural values that may not be our own. A healthy individual acts independent of what other people may think of him or her. This, of course, does not mean that you should do things just to be different or ignore the opinions of others. It does mean that above all else, tap into the wisdom of your Spiritual Self. Let your unique Spiritual Self unfold from within.

Your guidance is different than anyone else's. Your Spiritual Self will give you guidance that is unique for your own growth and wellbeing.

Step Three Exercises

1. *Think of a decision you need to make. In a notebook or journal, write down at least two options. Are you willing to accept any of these, even the ones that do not look appealing? If yes, which option would you choose if you were not afraid?*

2. *Write down under each option the reasons you think that a particular option is good or bad.*

3. *Get still and connect with your Spiritual Self.*

4. *Say each option aloud and write down the feelings you have in your body in response. Do any of the options give you sense of inner rightness, joy, or enthusiasm?*

5. *Discuss the options with a wise man or woman. Who might be intuitive yet impartial about the direction you should go in? Talk with them and be open to Spirit's guidance working through your conversation.*

6. *If an option is still not clear, choose the one that makes the most sense after following the above steps. Throughout the process, ask, "What's trying to happen here?" Be detached from any particular outcome, and open to what Source is seeking to do. Contentment and happiness in the now is independent of any particular outcome.*

7. *Keep a journal of the decisions you make. Learn from the results and develop your intuition in the process.*

8. *Take time each day to quiet your mind and connect with Source. Remain open to Spirit's direction even after taking action. The direction you are heading can be right for a while but Spirit may alter your course a bit. Always be open to Source's guidance.*

Step Four

Living in the Super Zone

"How little do we know of time, Alfred.
A one-syllable word, a noun.
Yesterday's laughter, tomorrow's tears."
—Batman (Adam West)

Living in the physical world can feel like the furthest thing from divinity. Feeding yourself, making money, nurturing relationships, and dealing with the other demands of your existence constitute a full-time effort. Your mind has endless occupations, and taking time to be spiritually minded seems impossible. **However, by living in a zone where God, or the Spiritual Self, resides, it is easier to have a direct communion with your inner spiritual guidance, and improve the quality of your existence. I refer to this living space as the Super Zone.**

We might have regrets of the past or worries about the future. However, life is happening right now and since we never know which moment is our last, we should live life to the fullest.

A Zen Parable

Two tigers chased a monk through the forest. The monk came to a cliff and shimmied down a vine to stop hundreds of feet from the ground. He looked down and saw that the tigers were waiting for him. He looked up and saw that a mouse was gnawing the top of the vine. Then he noticed a strawberry growing on the side of the cliff. The monk plucked the berry and ate it. That's living in the now.

❋ *You have 86,400 seconds each day. Do you fill these moments with regrets about the past or worries about the future? Next to each of the following statements, write T for true or F for false.*

❋ *I regret not going for a higher degree.*

❋ *I am worried about the state of the economy.*

❋ *I regret getting married and having children.*

❋ *I fear for my grandchild's future.*

❋ *I still think about something hurtful I said or did to someone in the past.*

❋ *I am worried about retirement.*

❋ *I am worried about global warming.*

❋ *I am angry with myself for eating that last piece of cake.*

✳ *Is there anything you can do right now about any of these situations?*
Apologize. Get a degree or a divorce. Walk around the block. Begin
a retirement savings plan. Start recycling.

When you are busy anticipating a better future, you fail to enjoy the good in the present moments. Though it is important to have dreams and goals and look forward to achieving them, remember that the only time we really have is the present moment.

We often fail to live in the now because we are conditioned to believe that our happiness comes from outside ourselves. We think that when we finally achieve or manifest something in the future, then we will have what our hearts long for and be happy. Living for the future means failing to experience the joy that could be yours right now.

Old Story

For centuries, human beings looked forward to a time after death when they will experience heaven, and their present moments will be filled with joy and peace. I do not believe that we automatically go to some place where life will suddenly be perfect. The experience of heaven is something that we are meant to experience *now*.

Frank Laubach experienced a bit of heaven every day. While serving as a missionary in the Philippines, he made it a practice to think about God once every minute whether by sending "flash prayers" to others in need, singing a verse from a hymn, repeating a Bible quote, or feeling Spirit's guidance. He recorded his experiences in a diary, later published as *Letters by a Modern Mystic*.

"This simple practice (thinking about God once a minute) requires only a gentle pressure of the will, not more than a person can exert easily. It grows easier as the habit becomes fixed. *Yet it transforms life into heaven. Everybody takes on a new richness, and all the world seems tinted with glory…the joy which I have within cannot be described. If there never were any other reward than that, it would more than justify the practice to me…"*

Laubach found the greatest secret of life: by consciously giving attention to Source, our present moments are more fulfilling and we can experience joy independent of what is or is not happening.

Concentrate On What You Are Doing

When asked how monks attained perfection, the Buddha answered: "When the monk walks he is fully in his walking, when he stands he is fully in his standing, when he sits down he is fully in his sitting down, and when he lies down he is fully in his lying down."

Yet we tend to talk when we eat, think when we walk, and quickly think about something different than what we were just thinking about. Our minds are seldom in the present moment.

Concentration is necessary for responding safely and effectively to the environment, and is also important to success in releasing our spiritual power. Anyone who concentrates his or her mind on a specific field of work is engaged in prayer and opens up to the flow of guidance. Mathematicians receive ideas about mathematics; teachers receive insights into their students; musicians receive lyrics for their songs; business people receive ideas for serving their customers. Concentrating the strands of your mind puts you in tune with a reservoir of wisdom and creativity from your Spiritual Self.

Psychologists write about what they call "flow," the state of mind in which you experience happiness and perform at outstanding levels. One of the characteristics of a person experiencing flow is intense concentration on what he or she is doing.

When athletes enter flow or "being in the zone," they perform at their maximum potential. Jane Blalock, a former player on the Ladies Professional Golf Association Tour, described what happened when she was fully concentrating: "It doesn't happen all the time, but when I'm playing well, sometimes it's as if my eyes change. I can feel it. I just feel like Dr. Jekyll and Mr. Hyde—a transformation happens, I'm a totally different human being. I don't hear anybody; I don't see anybody. Nothing bothers me; nothing is going to interfere with what I'm about to do."

When I'm totally engaged in speaking to an audience, I feel as if my eyes change. My eyes zoom in like a camera lens and people appear closer and more vivid. When this shift happens, sometimes I see light around a person, what is referred to as an aura. My heart becomes peaceful, and I am confident that my Spiritual Self is expressing. After I've had this experience, I've asked friends if they noticed a difference in my eyes or felt the presence of God when this visual shift happened, and they could. By turning attention to God or being an avenue for Spirit's expression, I release a form of energy that can be sensed by others.

When you fully concentrate your mind on what you are doing, you become an avenue through which Source, your Spiritual Self, is expressed. Gandhi wrote a letter to his secretary who was in jail, chastising him for learning French while on the spinning wheel. (Gandhi encouraged the use of the spinning wheel among the people of India as a symbol of self-sufficiency and independence from British rule.)

"I am disappointed that you still have not understood the meaning of the spinning wheel. We must give our full attention to whatever we are doing. Whatever we do, we must do with our whole mind and heart. Whatever you do, do it to perfection. When you are studying French, then study French, but by all means do not divide your attention studying French while operating the spinning wheel. I am pained that you have not realized the holiness of the spinning wheel as well as everything we do."

Practice the Art of Blessing

According to *Webster's Dictionary*, to bless is "to honor or praise; to confer prosperity or well-being." When you bless someone or something, you are beholding the spiritual dimension and living in the Super Zone.

One Sunday morning while riding in a bus from New Jersey to Manhattan's Port Authority Bus Terminal, a man sitting in front of me began talking loudly on his cell phone. When I pointed out the sign at the front of the bus that read, "No Cell Phones," he shouted an obscenity and said, "Somebody's about to get slapped." I was tempted to argue with him, but instead began to silently bless him: "Divine love flowing through me blesses you." I also said the prayer for protection (the man was about six foot three and weighed over two hundred pounds): "The light of God surrounds me. The love of God enfolds me. The power of God protects me. The presence of God watches over me. Wherever I am, God is, and all is well." Not long after, he turned around in his seat and in a calm voice said: "I apologize for my behavior. I overreacted."

Use the power of blessing on others by imagining light streaming from between your eyebrows, your spiritual eye, to the same point in the other person. When you are self-conscious in talking with someone, shift attention from your self by consciously imagining bathing him or her in spiritual light or sending love or peace from your heart. Sending energy to the higher self of another person is important to your spiritual evolution.

A Smile for Clara

Every morning, Clara rode the subway to work. Another woman always seemed to be in a negative mood and placed a bag on the seat next to hers so no one could sit there. One morning, Clara was inspired to silently bless the woman. Suddenly, she gave Clara a big smile, moved her bag out of the way, and offered Clara the seat.

Take a moment before eating to bless your food. Sixteen years ago, I saw a demonstration by a man using dousing rods. He used the rods to measure the energy fields of people and food prior to and after blessing them. Blessing the food caused the rods to indicate an increased frequency of energy. Since then, I bless my food, and this enhances its vitality and nourishment.

Bless your clothes as you dress so that you realize that you are being constantly clothed with Spirit's substance. If shopping is low on your priority list as it is mine, perhaps blessing your clothes will make them last longer.

Bless your physical body, each organ and function. Norman Vincent Peale, author of *The Power of Positive Thinking*, blessed the cells of his body every morning and as a result had a constant source of energy.

Repeat Sacred Words and Phrases

You can also access your Super Zone through the repetition of a sacred phrase, such as "I am centered and poised in the peace of God," or words like love, joy, God, Shalom, Jesus, Om, Beloved, Father, and Mother. As you repeat a word, you can feel a quickening of energy and joy flowing in your brain.

Swami Muktananda said: "Catching a glimpse of the beauty of reality is a gift made possible…through the power of repeating God's name, whether through chanting, prayer, or mantra repetition."

Repeat your word or phrase while you are walking, exercising, folding laundry, or washing dishes. Repeating a sacred word keeps your mind focused in a positive manner, rather than roving into negative or fearful thoughts.

We are bombarded by countless messages on a daily basis, many of which are not in our highest interest. Protect yourself from negative subconscious influences by chanting aloud a mantra to create a spiritual energy field. Repeating a sacred word can protect you from various kinds of pollution: air, unwanted advertising, and negative people's vibrations.

Keep a chart to support you in practicing the presence of Spirit. On one axis, write down routine activities that you do during the day—getting your car keys, taking a shower, brushing teeth, and feeding the pet. Whenever you do any of these activities, repeat your sacred word or phrase. At the end of the day, put a check mark next to the activity in which you remembered to repeat your sacred word. Fill out the chart until you develop the habit.

While living and working at the Ananda Meditation Retreat in Northern California, I participated in a two-month spiritual training program. Each morning we performed selfless service. We cleaned bathrooms, painted, and did whatever could be done during an hour. Every fifteen minutes, someone would ring a gong, reminding us to focus our attention on Spirit as we worked, which was referred to as practicing the Presence. I was amazed at how elevated I felt while performing these tasks that I previously considered a mere chore.

I often silently repeat a sacred word while playing golf. Initially, I resisted the practice because I was on the golf course to relax, let go of mental activity, and enjoy the outdoors. However, there were times when I was not enjoying myself but was frustrated. Through repeating the sacred word I have discovered a new joy in golf whether I'm playing well or not. Some of my best performances have been when I was practicing the Source.

As you repeat your sacred word, bring your awareness to the point between the eyebrows. Yogi mystics say that this point is the spiritual center in the body where you can make contact with your Spiritual Self.

Add a song to your repetition and create your own powerful chant. Chanting will help open the heart's natural love and longing for God. Sing a spiritual song or chant a verse repeatedly and eventually you will feel love and joy in your heart.

Songs

- ❊ *How Great Thou Art*
- ❊ *You'll Never Walk Alone*
- ❊ *In the Garden*
- ❊ *Joy Down in My Heart*
- ❊ *Amazing Grace*

Chants

- ❊ *I am the bubble, make me the sea,*
  So do Thou my Lord: Thou and I, never apart.
  Wave of the sea, dissolve in the sea!
  I am the bubble, make me the sea,
  Make me the sea, oh, make me the sea!

- ❊ *My Lord, I will be Thine always.*
  I may go far, farther than the stars,
  But I will be Thine always, my Lord

Devotees may come, devotees may go,
But I will be Thine always, my Lord.

Chant for World Peace

✻ *Auspiciousness be unto all,*
Perfect peace be unto all,
Fullness be unto all,
Prosperity be unto all.
Happiness be unto all,
Perfect health be unto all,
May all see good in everyone,
May all be free from suffering.

Feel Spirit Expressed Through You

At the Vipassana Meditation Retreat, students participate in outdoor walking meditations. In one such meditation, each chose a strip of land about fifteen yards long and proceeded to walk that strip back and forth to feel the subtle movements of our steps without thinking of anything else. This is an excellent practice for becoming aware of the flow of Spirit's power through the physical body.

Whenever I speak to an audience, I enter the Super Zone by considering myself an instrument of God. Sometimes I am guided by intuition to talk about certain topics that I had not prepared. Afterward, attendees tell me that particular vignette was exactly what they needed to hear. Cases like this show the Spiritual Self expressing through me. By consciously being in the Super Zone, I allow it to express in a way that benefits the highest good for everyone.

Practice the Presence in Nature

One way to practice seeing God in the world around you is to let nature be a reminder of Spirit's presence. Physicists say that the material world is condensed energy. This energy is a manifestation of Spirit. Whatever beauty you see in the world around you is a reflection of the Source of all beauty. Feel the wind and think, "Spirit, you are the wind beneath my wings." See the butterfly and think of your Spiritual Self awakening within the cocoon of your humanness. See the swaying tree and think of going with the flow of Spirit.

Part of Creation

A woman who had been kayaking talked with a man on the shore. She told him that she was a workaholic until she was diagnosed with cancer. When she went into treatment, she took time to camp, hike, and kayak. Part of her healing process had been to recognize that she's not running the show. In her kayak she sat low and close to the water, feeling that she was part of the boat, the water, and the sky, the whole mystery of creation.

See God Expressing As You

When you get up in the morning, look in the mirror. Center yourself and enter the Super Zone by acknowledging that the person looking back at you is an expression of God. You are God *being* you.

Philosophers since Aristotle have said that what we want above all else is to be happy. Happiness is possible in each moment when we give our attention to the source of joy and know that it resides within us. Living in the Super Zone by practicing the presence of Spirit not only uplifts you, but also has a positive influence on all humanity.

In his book *Power vs. Force*, Dr. David Hawkins writes: "In this interconnected Universe, every improvement we make in our private world improves the world at large for everyone." Hawkins has scientifically demonstrated that people as well as groups vibrate at different frequencies of energy. He found that eighty-seven percent of people vibrate at energy levels that weaken them. He writes: *"One individual who lives and vibrates to the energy of optimism and a willingness to be nonjudgmental of others will counterbalance the negativity of 90,000 individuals who calibrate at the lower weakening levels."*

When you focus your attention on the Spiritual Self within, you are affecting the consciousness of humanity.

See God Expressing As Others

The more we are able to accept ourselves as expressions of Spirit, the more we are able to accept the sacredness of others. Mother Teresa looked on the people she helped in the streets of Calcutta as "Jesus in disguise." Every person is Spirit.

In a speech class in college, we were given the assignment to interview and introduce a student to the rest of the class. The student I was paired with made curt remarks and laughed deridingly instead of cooperating. I fought back the tendency to react negatively, and instead thought of her as "Jesus in disguise."

Her demeanor changed right before my eyes. She relaxed, and spoke warmly and cheerfully. When it was her turn to ask me questions, she listened with rapt attention. From that time on, whenever I saw her on campus, she greeted me as if we had been best friends for years.

While working as a cashier at the Ananda Spiritual Retreat Center, I was conscious of seeing a customer I'll call Stan as an expression of Spirit. Stan suddenly stopped, looked at me in a curious manner, and said in a reverent tone: "No one has ever looked at me as you are right now." Simply by acknowledging a person's spiritual nature, we can have a positive influence on him or her.

Be aware of Spirit acting in all things. Make the effort to hear what Spirit is saying to you through a person's words or nonverbal clues. Imagine Spirit looking at you through the eyes of another. Ask yourself, "What is Spirit saying to me through this person?"

When you practice the presence of God, you live in the Super Zone of fulfillment and happiness. "Thou wilt keep him in perfect peace, whose mind is stayed on thee: because he trusteth in thee." (Isaiah 26:3)

Step Four Exercise

1. Remind yourself of the benefits of practicing the presence of God. Write on an index card your commitment to be aware of Spirit and what it will do for you and others. Place these notes on your refrigerator, computer, or bathroom mirror.

I once wrote: "What my heart longs for more than anything else and what I believe is the purpose of life is to become aware of the presence of God. Today I live each moment to the fullest by keeping my mind on Spirit as often as possible, which causes everything else to unfold according to God's plan, which blesses others as well. The greatest contribution I can make to humanity today is practicing the presence of God."

Step Five

Your Secret Hideout

"When thou prayest, enter into thy closet, and
when thou hast shut thy door, pray to thy Father
which is in secret…"
—Matthew 6:6

The "closet" in the above quote is the place of solitude within where you can recharge your mind, body, and soul. In almost every spiritual tradition, there is a method of quieting the mind and entering the stillness within. This practice of stilling the mind is often referred to as meditation.

By meditating, we tune out of worldly consciousness and into the realm of Spirit. In addition to living a virtuous life, practice concentration and meditation, which will lead you to experiencing your Spiritual Self. In that state, you can actually experience God.

On a more physical and mental level, meditation quiets the limbic system of the brain, which is responsible for emotions such as fear, rage, and aggression. Simultaneously, meditation stimulates the prefrontal lobes, the part of the brain located above the eyebrows that is responsible for qualities such as idealism, joy, focus, creativity, and abstract thought. Those who meditate have been found to experience less anxiety and depression and have greater self-control, enhanced social skills, and better management of anger.

The Power of Meditation

Kiran Bedi was in charge of the prison system in India. She worried that the prisoners were not being treated like human beings and would commit violent crimes soon after release.

A guard told her about a form of meditation that had changed him from a violent person to a peaceful one. Bedi was intrigued and offered the prisoners a ten-day silent retreat to practice this meditation. Twelve hundred prisoners participated, including Christians, Muslims, and Hindus. "It made my prisoners weep," she said. "They looked within themselves and saw the feeling of revenge. They saw their anger and the hurt they had caused society, and wanted to be different."

Scientific Proof of the Benefits of Meditation

There are many scientifically validated benefits of going within. Peter Suedfeld of the University of British Columbia conducted an experiment called restricted environmental stimulation therapy (REST), which consisted of going into a completely dark and soundless room and lying on a bed. The participants were provided with food, water, and everything else that they needed. They were able to shut off the outer world and find deep inner rest. The participants used REST to overcome weight problems, reduce alcohol consumption, decrease stress, overcome irrational fears, and increase their self-confidence.

Treating Social Anxiety With Meditation

The National Institute of Mental Health has funded a $2.5 million five-year study at Stanford University to help people calm their social anxiety that affects seven percent of American adults. The study uses non-drug approaches such as meditation, which is free from the side effects of weight gain and grogginess caused by drugs.

Further scientific proof has been shown through experiments measuring the level of happiness in Buddhist monks, who engage in extensive meditation. The experiments were run by Richard Davidson, director of the Laboratory for Affective Neuroscience at the University of Wisconsin, who had discovered a method for determining a person's typical mood range by reading the levels of activity in the right and left parts of the brain. When the ratio tilts to the right, the more unhappy or distressed a person tends to be. More activity in the left side shows a happier and more enthusiastic person.

Davidson tested the right-left ratio on a senior Tibetan lama, who turned out to have the most extreme left value of the 175 people measured. Davidson believes the practice of meditation is the reason.

He also conducted brain scans of both novice meditators and Buddhist monks who had spent more than ten thousand hours in meditation. Scans of the monks showed much higher brain activity than the novices. The monks' brains also showed greater stimulation at the sight of suffering, coupled with a stronger urge to alleviate that suffering. The findings of these experiments strongly suggest that mental training such as meditation alters the structure and function of the brain.

But you don't need to become a Buddhist monk to reap the benefits of meditation. Davidson conducted a test involving workers from a high-profile biotech business who meditated for three hours a week over a two-month period. Prior to the training, the workers' brain activity tipped toward the right. They also complained of high stress.

After the training, their emotional ratio on average shifted leftward, toward the positive zone. In addition, their moods improved. They were more engaged in their work, more energized, and less anxious. The results suggest that meditation will block stressful emotions and release positive emotions in the brain.

Meditation as a Spiritual Experience

Many never experience their Spiritual Self because they spend their lifetime learning *about* God and rarely directly experience God by learning to quiet their mind. Ralph Waldo Emerson, the transcendental philosopher, said, "When we have broken with the God of tradition, and ceased from the God of the intellect, then God fires us with his presence."

Knowing the Mango

A group of scientists who didn't know anything about mangoes wanted to understand what a mango is. A committee visited a mango orchard. Some members analyzed the fruit's size, shape, scent, and color. Others studied the mango tree itself, how the trunk was formed and the root structures.

At one point, they noticed that one of their committee was missing. They spotted him lying on a rock in the sun eating mangoes. He knew what a mango was. He went beyond intellectual analysis and tasted the mango firsthand.

Meditation is the art of stilling the mind in order to access the Spiritual Self. With meditation, new grooves are formed in the brain, and the mind moves upward in the new spiritual grooves. Swami Sivananda Saraswati said, "Meditation is the only royal road…a mysterious ladder which reaches from earth to heaven, from error to truth, from darkness to light, from pain to bliss, from restlessness to abiding peace, from ignorance to knowledge…"

Why More People Should Meditate

If there are such great benefits to meditation, how come more people don't take up the practice? *Many of us are distracted by outer things and need to realize that our deepest longing is to connect with Spirit.*

My experience in teaching people how to meditate is that though many have read about the importance of meditation and taken courses, they still do not know how to do it. Some have said they have tried and are not good at the practice. They may be better off engaging in another method of contemplation. However, most people are equipped for and would benefit greatly from the daily practice of meditation.

Refrain from labeling any of your efforts at meditating as "bad." Any sincere effort made to quiet your mind, to experience your connection with Source, is beneficial.

Being still is a skill, like playing the piano or learning to play golf. You must practice. The more you practice, the better you will get at quieting your mind and discovering the bliss within.

Learning to meditate is about mastering your mind. Your training in meditation will serve in many areas of your life. When you are persistent, you will feel a greater sense of calmness and joy in *all* your activities.

With meditation, you can check certain negative emotions and impulses, feel more in touch with your intuition, have greater clarity of mind and quicker reflexes, and bask in a greater sense of wellbeing.

From Complaint to Compliment

Linda learned these meditation techniques in a workshop, and was asked what meditation had done for her. She said, "A deeper sense of peace, and that is no small thing." Linda works for a real estate company. She is one of four employees with eighty agents. She works with the finances as well as marketing. She continued, "Meditation has also enabled me to remain objective and not get sucked into the drama." One such drama occurred when an agent complained to her about seagull droppings on his new car while he was showing a million dollar mansion. Remaining objective, Linda said, "You are so lucky, Bob. You live near the ocean where there are seagulls. How wonderful that you have a new car and seagulls do what they do." Bob turned to Linda and said, "You're right. I am lucky."

While there are many wonderful meditation practices, I have included the basic principles in the appendix, "Meditation for Beginners," to help you in making meditation a daily habit.

Remaining Steadfast

Meditation is a very important spiritual practice. The *Bhagavad Gita* says: "A little practice of this inward religion will free you from dire fears and colossal sufferings." The "inward religion" is realizing your connection with your Spiritual Self.

Meditating on a regular basis changes your life. You will find the strength you need to go through any challenge, and **radiate greater peace and calmness that people will feel in your presence.** Therefore, make a commitment to your daily practice of meditation.

Through a direct experience of Spirit in meditation, you release your potential, the Spiritual Self. The more time you take to become still and move beyond words and thoughts in meditation, you allow these spiritual qualities to emerge in and through you, and become part of your daily expression.

A Gradual Transformation

Consider the process of dyeing a white cloth by immersing it into a vat of red dye. The first time the cloth is dipped into the dye and removed, it is as bright red as the dye in the vat. Once the cloth dries, however, it becomes nearly white again, with little color remaining. As the process of dipping the cloth in the dye and allowing it to dry continues, the cloth becomes a little redder until eventually it is the same rich color as the dye.

Like the cloth, the more often you dip your self in the dye of Spirit's presence by entering your secret hideout of meditation, the more you will express the fruits of Spirit and tap into your Spiritual Self.

Step Five Exercises

1. *Now that you have learned what meditation is and why it's important, it is time to develop the habit. Look at your daily schedule and decide on a time to practice meditation for five minutes. Write a note and post this in a conspicuous place, like the refrigerator or bathroom mirror.*

2. *Pick a location in your home that is conducive to being still, such as a corner in the bedroom. Have a chair without arms that enables you to sit upright.*

3. *Create an altar to support you in feeling uplifted. Use a small table and choose items that have meaning for you: photographs of enlightened teachers or loved ones, shells from the seaside, candles, and an incense burner.*

4. *Now you are ready to begin one of the most important and enriching spiritual activities. See the appendix, "Meditation for Beginners" to learn practical techniques and tips. Enjoy the process, and remember that there is no such thing as a bad meditation. Just keep at it.*

5. *For more information on how to deepen your meditation practice and receive additional support with meditation, go to www.superyoubook.com/bookbonus.*

Step Six

Super Healing

"Then shall thy light break forth as the morning,
and thine health shall spring forth speedily."
—Isaiah 58:8

Bill is an ideal example of our innate power to create wholeness. Doctors told Bill that he would be a hemiplegic—paralyzed on one side—for the rest of his life after a near-fatal head injury during the Vietnam War. He had been thrown out of a jeep and landed on the ground headfirst, smashing his brain against bone. Doctors had to drill holes in his skull to prevent deadly swelling. After the surgery, Bill was in a deep coma. The Army had sent his family a telegram informing them that he would most likely not recover.

Bill did wake up from the coma, but found himself paralyzed on his left side. He was given the prognosis that he would never walk again. Confused and angry, Bill made up his mind that he would overcome the doctors' decree. He knew of the innate power to create health and wholeness, and tapped into it by believing one hundred percent in his ability to heal.

When Bill first tried to walk, he fell down. Still he kept try-ing and believing. He also exercised his paralyzed left arm with weights and the same intensity of belief.

A few months later, Bill walked out of the Walter Reed Army Medical Center. Not only could Bill walk and move his left arm, but he also went on to become a body-builder and marathon runner.

Bill said, "Miracles like mine are available to everyone. I am no different. All anyone needs is to KNOW that complete recovery from illness and injury is possible. As long as you believe it and do what is necessary to regain that which you lost to injury or illness, anything is possible. I am a perfect example of this. This is the truth as I know it." He shared his story with me during a round of golf while walking and carrying his clubs.

Health is our natural state, and the body continually does what-ever it can to restore itself to wholeness. Real health comes from within. *A spiritual pattern, a divine blueprint, is inside every person. This pattern is always complete regardless of what may be going on in the physical body.*

When you are not aware of your natural health, you block the life flow and problems occur. If a rubber band is placed on a finger and cuts off the circulation, eventually the finger will swell, turn blue, and is lost. The rubber band must be removed to allow for proper circulation. Similarly, your thoughts, beliefs, and behavior patterns need to be in harmony with the natural circulation of life force in the body.

Healing takes place within the body every day in a variety of ways. Symptoms of a cold or a blemish on the skin disappear. An upset stomach is soothed, a cut on the finger mends, a nose stops running, and a fever temperature returns to normal.

Stress is one of the major ways that we disconnect from our innate wholeness and block such healing. *A wise doctor said: "Illness is not simply a matter of what you are eating, but also what's eating you."* Anything that you can do to decrease unhealthy stress contributes to your health.

Desire to be Well

Some people use their illness to make a connection with other people. Their wounds are a source of power to manipulate others. You may know people who have not carried out certain commitments they were capable of, using their wounds as an excuse.

Jesus met a man who had been sitting by the pool at Bethesda for thirty-eight years. The man complained that no one had ever helped him get into the healing waters of the pool. Jesus asked him: "Do you want to be healed?" Jesus could see that the man had not yet wanted to be healed, but he had reached a point where he was sick and tired of being sick and tired. Jesus said: "Rise, take up thy bed and walk," (John 5:8) and the man did.

Ask yourself if you desire to be healed, or if you rely on your wounds as a source of power. It is important that you continue to grow and discover your inner strength. Then you can respond to your Spiritual Self when it asks if you want to be healed with a definite "yes."

Have Faith In Your Wholeness

With faith, you can look beyond the condition of your body and behold the wholeness that was created in your spiritual blueprint of perfection.

A woman suffered from a hemorrhage for twelve years. She sought out Jesus, thinking that if she touched his garment, she would be made well. He turned to her and said: "Daughter, be of good comfort; thy faith hath made thee whole." (Matthew 9:22) Through faith, she looked beyond the appearance of her illness and became aware of the presence of God as wholeness, and she was healed.

The Perfection of a Rose

Sasha, a native of Russia, had suffered a hand injury while in the middle of a battle between her cat and a dog she was trying to rescue from the street. Her hand was full of bloody scratches, and when she awoke the next morning, it was swollen and blue in color. She couldn't move it. Sasha was immediately hospitalized for blood poisoning. Three days later, her entire arm had swollen and was blue up to her shoulder. She was put in a room with people scheduled for amputations.

Sasha refused to believe that her arm would be amputated. One of her friends brought her three red roses, which were very expensive in Russia. Sasha loved roses and spent the evening looking at them. Around two in the morning, she felt a sense of oneness with the life energy that she saw in the flowers. Afterward, she felt a kind of release and went to sleep.

The next morning, the doctor and his assistants awakened Sasha. The swelling was gone in her arm and the color had returned to normal. She was completely healed. The doctor, who had been ready to amputate, looked at her arm and said, "Sometimes the penicillin takes a little time to work." Right.

Thich Nhat Hanh, a Buddhist monk and author of *Peace Is Every Step*, said: "When we look at a flower, we can see the whole cosmos contained in it. One petal is the whole of the flower and the whole of the Universe." By giving her attention to the perfection of the roses, Sasha released the wholeness of the Spirit within her.

By the way, the dog did get rescued, and the friend who brought the roses later became Sasha's husband and the father of their two children.

Be Steadfast

If you accept your innate wholeness with complete faith and open up the channels through which healing life can flow, you can be healed instantly. However, sometimes you need to be steadfast and persistent in developing that faith. You may still need the help of something outside of yourself such as traditional medicine or holistic methods to assist in bringing you back to wholeness.

Healing With Faith

After much deliberation, Beth decided to leave a ten-year marriage and take a job across the country. Full of hope and promise, she thought she was making a change for the better and looked forward to starting a new life.

Soon afterwards she suffered a stroke that left her with a number of handicaps. She had been a newspaper editor but could no longer compose a sentence. She was unable to walk, clothe, or feed herself. The medicine she took bloated her face. Her hands quivered and she tired very easily. Beth fell unconscious at times, and had to wear a tag attached to her blouse to identify herself. She cried in desperation when people who were trying to help could not understand what she was saying.

Eventually, with a lot of therapy, Beth was able to write affirmations for perfect health. She never wavered in her desire to be healed and in her steadfast faith that she would recover.

Through consistent effort and ongoing belief, Beth made tremendous strides in recovery, and went on to fulfill her heart's desire to get a master's degree in sociology. Today she is happily married to the man of her dreams. Last time I saw Beth, she looked radiant and healthy.

* *Sometimes the only way to reach your spiritual potential is through a trying experience that forces you to exercise your faith. However, you don't have to wait for adversity to develop steadfast faith. You can begin right now. Below is a list of the ways you can develop your faith.*

* *Read a daily devotional such as "The Daily Word" and reflect on how you can apply the ideas to your life.*

* *Take a few minutes at the beginning of the day to visualize how you would like certain events to unfold.*

* *At the close of the day, reflect with gratitude for the blessings of good that occurred.*

* *When you think of a loved one, see them happy, peaceful, and know that they are guided and protected.*

* *Listen and follow your intuition in small ways (see step three, "Super Guidance").*

* *When faced with a challenge, pause for a deep breath, and affirm to yourself, "Everything is working together for good because God is in charge."*

Forgive

To experience wholeness, forgiveness is essential. It is easy to feel righteous and believe that you are standing your ground by being unforgiving. However, even if you are right in a certain situation, not forgiving an offense can actually hurt you. Resentment, bitterness, and hatred can block the energetic flow of life in the body, and create disease.

Right to be Angry

Barbara developed a lump in her breast. Through self-inquiry and prayer, she realized that she was still holding on to her anger and bitterness about her husband's infidelity some years earlier. Even though she was right to be angry, the hardness in her mind created the hardness in her body. When Barbara truly forgave her husband, the lump dissolved.

A few years ago I developed painful kidney stones. This was surprising since I eat healthy, drink lots of water, and exercise regularly. Shortly after the diagnosis, I had the urge to write about a negative incident that happened with a person the year before. Anger and bitterness poured out onto the page with an intensity I hadn't realized was there. As challenging as it was, I wholeheartedly forgave the person and stuck the letter in a drawer. A few days later, the kidney stone easily passed through my body.

It is easier to see the speck in your neighbor's eye than the log in your own eye, and point the finger at someone else instead of seeing your own shortcomings. *Evaluate every situation of blame with a discriminating mind, and discover if your own weakness played any part in it.*

Are there any patterns in your life that keep repeating? This is an indication of something that needs attention. For example, you have had problems with your bosses at various jobs. Instead of writing them off as jerks, consider that there may be something within you that is influencing your relationships at work. You tap into your Spiritual Self by engaging in self-inquiry and taking steps to work on your developmental needs as you become aware of them. Then, of course, you need to forgive your self.

Your willingness to forgive is most important. Sometimes, you may be hesitant to forgive because you don't like certain people or what they have done. You may feel righteous in your resentment. This bitterness is still detrimental to your health and wholeness. Resentment is like swallowing a poison and expecting the other person to die. *It is not necessary to like the other person or condone his or her actions to forgive.* You can love these people with an impersonal sense of goodwill.

Sometimes it's very difficult to forgive. How can we forgive a drunk driver or a rapist who has hurt us, or somebody close to us? Forgiveness when it is difficult can be found by turning the other cheek. Turn away from your human self that is bound to ego and limitation, and choose the Spiritual Self within where divine love dwells.

Living Her Faith

Poet and visionary Dr. Maya Angelou's son was hit by a drunk driver while living in the African bush. This landed him in a hospital with a broken neck, arm, and leg. Not only were his injuries severe, the hospital had few modern comforts and technology to alleviate his suffering. Dr. Angelou spent many sleepless nights by his bedside, praying for his healing and coming to terms with what had happened to her son.

The man who caused her son's condition came to visit them in the hospital. He was cheerful and casual as if he did not comprehend the seriousness of the situation, and as if his drunkenness was not directly responsible. Suspecting he was drunk again, Dr. Angelou froze him out, and spoke few words.

After he left, Dr. Angelou's son called her quietly to the foot of his bed. He whispered, "Mother, did you mean what you've told me and what we've studied? Is this man also a child of God?" He reminded her that even the bruisers and batterers of this world were children of God, whom she needed to forgive in order to live her faith. In the days that followed, she genuinely welcomed the man into her home.

Recognize the essential unity in all creatures, and know that if we are all one, we are spiritually connected even to the drunk driver and the rapist. By forgiving the perpetrator, we forgive and heal ourselves.

In our human form, we cannot know what our soul and the souls of others need for growth. We cannot know the state of consciousness of others, or their possible traumatic past. Therefore, we cannot judge well their actions. But what we can do is take control of our own spiritual growth. Jesus said that we must forgive "seventy times seven." (Matthew 18:22) Forgive indefinitely until you are free of the negative emotions that block you from experiencing the Spiritual Self.

Be Still

Through stillness, you can move beyond the physical body and experience the spiritual dimension of your being. Stillness can be a form of regeneration for the body through the receiving of spiritual energy, or life force.

Whenever the body is ill, it often craves rest—a waiting period. "Wait" is derived from the Hebrew word *qavah*, which means, "to bind together." ***When you quiet your mind and turn within, recharging and waiting for spiritual guidance, you bind your self to the Spirit that is our innate wholeness and perfection.*** The result may be an immediate healing, or you may be guided to a doctor, physical therapist, chiropractor, or holistic treatment.

The Miracle of Spirit

My friend Dorothy has spent a lot of time in meditation, focusing her attention on the words, "I am Spirit." She e-mailed me after the following experience that occurred while she prepared dinner. "While taking a cookie sheet out of the oven (450 degrees) with a small terrycloth towel—I know I should have been using my oven mitts, but wasn't—the towel caught fire and the flames went up my right hand. I dropped the towel on the floor and put the hot cookie sheet on the cutting board, picked up the flaming towel and tossed it in the sink, all within seconds, and with a yell to Ron [her husband] who was at the other end of the house in the TV room. He came running. The cotton friendship bracelet on my wrist was smoldering, and he immediately cut it off. We always have a large jar of aloe vera in the refrigerator for just such emergencies. Within seconds I had my entire hand in a large cup of the juice, and leaned over with my head almost on the counter, either with pain or shock, and experienced pain like I had never had before.

As I quivered, not knowing whether I was going to pass out or throw up, all of a sudden seemingly from the medulla area [hollow cavity at the base of the skull] and going up inside my head to the top were the words, '*I am Spirit.*' It was automatic, and even though the hurting was so bad, the words kept on and on. I was finally able to stand and sit in a chair with my hand still in the aloe, and pick at my supper. Ron gently wrapped my hand in a soft cloth (from an old bedspread from his Mom's house that he happened to find) soaked in aloe and covered with a plastic bag to keep it on for the night. I took a couple of Tylenol, as it was still very painful, and went to bed and had a decent night's sleep.

Now for the *miracle*—when we took off the still damp cloth the next morning, we expected to see blisters. There was nothing but a little redness on the tips of two fingers and not one bit of soreness. It is so amazing that I wanted to share with you that the years of different affirmations, usually including words like, 'I am Spirit' sure worked some kind of wonderful thing. I suggest you push the 'I am Spirit' bit a lot! It came through for me quite spontaneously when in a bit of trouble and pain. Part of me wishes I had a movie of the whole thing, as I, in retrospect, have *never* been that close to hot flames, and I can see my hand this morning and it is perfect. I know that *wherever we are God is*, and how good and useful, not to exclude comforting, strong affirmations can be when they kick in spontaneously."

When you take time to be still and connect with your innate wholeness, you will also be guided to do what is best in the situation (see step five, "Your Secret Hideout").

Direct the Life Force

Mystics and metaphysicians have taught through the ages that the Universe has only one mind. That mind is omnipresent, and also in every cell of your body.

Scientists such as Candace Pert have found that cells throughout your body think, not just those in your brain. Our thoughts communicate directly with all the organs in your body. Therefore, what you think about and focus on is critical to what you experience.

Paramhansa Yogananda taught that the greater the will and focus, the greater the flow of energy. He said that you are surrounded by cosmic energy that enters the nervous system through the medulla oblongata, the hollow cavity at the base of the brain, and becomes the life force.

This life force renews and restores the structures of your cells. Just as the battery of a car not only needs water but also electric charge, so does your body need more than food and water; your body needs the electric charge of the life force. Yogananda taught how to use your will to direct this force to the areas of the body that need healing.

Myrtle Fillmore, the cofounder of the Unity movement, was

sickly much of her life. At forty, she was diagnosed with tuberculosis and given six months to live. Instead of giving in, she studied the healing miracles of Jesus and principles for directing the life force. After seven years, she was completely healed and went on to live another active and vigorous forty years.

* *Direct the healing life force by imagining that you are breathing in energy through the medulla oblongata, filling your lungs with light. Now imagine directing the light to the cells and organs of your body, healing and restoring them.*

* *Sit upright in a chair and take a few long, slow, deep breaths. As you exhale, imagine that you are letting go of tension held in the muscles of your body. Scan each muscle from the bottoms of your feet to the top of your head and send the message to each muscle, "relax and let go."*

* *Once you are relaxed, place your right hand on the back of your head and feel the hollow cavity at the base of the skull. This is the medulla oblongata. This is where you imagine the light will fill your lungs as you take a deep breath.*

* *Place your hand back in your lap. Take a long, deep breath and imagine the energy emanating from the medulla is filling your lungs with light as you inhale. While breathing normally, imagine this light radiating to each organ in your body.*

* *With the power of intention, visualize this light healing, renewing and restoring to wholeness each organ and function of your body. After a little while, sit still for a minute. Open your eyes and trust*

that God's healing light is at work in your body, restoring it to
wholeness and perfection. Be aware of how Spirit directs you to
foster and support the healing taking place inside.

Do Not Judge Yourself Because of Illness

There are many people who believe they will never get sick if
they are spiritually minded. However, many spiritual masters
have experienced illness. The Buddha is said to have died
from food poisoning, having been fed tainted meat in what
became his final meal. Saint Bernadette, who saw the vision
of the Virgin at Lourdes in 1858, where thousands of people
have reportedly been healed, died of bone cancer at the age
of thirty-five. Suzuki Roshi, who brought Zen Buddhism from
Japan to the United States and established the San Francisco
Zen Center, died from cancer of the liver. Sri Ramana Maha-
rishi, perhaps the most beloved saint of modern India, died
from cancer of the stomach.

Jesus came across a man who had been blind from birth.
His disciples asked him: "Master, who did sin, this man, or his
parents, that he was born blind?" (John 9:2) Jesus answered:
"Neither hath this man sinned, nor his parents: but that the
works of God should be made manifest in him." (John 9:3).
Jesus looked at the man's blindness as an opportunity to give
expression to his innate wholeness.

The mystic Edgar Cayce often received insight into others' illnesses and steps they could take to experience healing.
Cayce said that in many instances, people experienced a serious

physical illness as a result of their consciousness from two or three lifetimes ago. This is a good reason to not judge yours or any other person's spiritual development because of their physical condition. Notice that Jesus did not rebuke his disciples for implying that the blind man had lived a previous incarnation where he may have sinned. Instead Jesus focused on what the man could do today, experience his innate wholeness.

Rather than blaming and judging your self for what you are experiencing physically, look at the experience as an opportunity to grow and express your wholeness. One of the lessons many have learned through illness is that we are not our bodies. We are whole spiritual beings, regardless of what challenges may happen with our bodies. An ancient text of India talks about "that part of the body fire cannot burn, wind cannot dry, water cannot wet, weapons cannot cleave." That is our spiritual body, the Spirit within.

The Lessons of Illness

In 1988, Minister Happy Winingham was an avid marathon runner. However, she started to feel very weak and learned that she had contracted AIDS from a former boyfriend. Happy did everything she could think of to heal herself. She tried different types of holistic therapies and healing treatments. Even so, two years later she contracted the flu, which resulted in spinal meningitis to the brain.

Happy was in intensive care and in excruciating pain, because the brain was swollen and the spinal cord infected. At one point, Happy did not have any blood pressure and her extremities were dying because the energy was withdrawing to her inner core. She asked the nurse to give her five minutes of silence, and the nurse agreed to give her only two because of her condition.

During those two minutes, Happy's kidneys failed and she felt as if the veils of life were lifting. Happy had been building a home where she was going to live with her friends and their twelve-year-old daughter. She wondered what would happen to that dream. She also wondered what would happen to her ministry. A voice said to her: "It will be taken care of."

She felt a strong, joyful presence all around her. The voice said to her: "You see, I had to take you to the end of life. I had to take everything away from you before you could realize that it is my will that you are alive... Remember what this love feels like because this love and this joy are available to you all of the time... It is you who are putting the veils in front of your eyes, preventing you from feeling this joy and a disease-free consciousness continuously. Remember what this feels like."

Happy learned from her experience with AIDS that she was not her body, but a spiritual being. She almost died on two other occasions. When asked what kept her going, she responded: "Knowing that love is with me all the time. There is not any suffering unless I create it."

Happy died in 1998. Her funeral was attended by hundreds of people who had been helped and inspired by her life. Though her body never completely healed, her soul had, and she contributed to the healing of many others.

Experience Joy and Love

"A merry heart doeth good like a medicine." (Proverbs 17:22) Science has demonstrated a definite connection between a person's level of joy and their physical wellbeing.

Your body is capable of producing the healing chemicals that you need in the right dosage, at the right time, targeted to the right organs, with no side effects. The emotion of exhilaration produces health-inducing chemicals in the body such as Interleukin, used in the treatment of cancer. A prescription for Interleukin-2 costs $40,000. However, you can produce millions of dollars of Interleukin by engaging in an activity that brings you the feeling of exhilaration.

* *What gives you a sense of great joy?*

* *Hiking*

* *Bicycle riding*

* *Going to the movies*

* *Playing golf*

* *Making love*

* *Reading a good book*

* *Talking with your best friend*

* *Meditation*

✳ *Going to church*

✳ *Listening to music*

✳ *Dancing*

✳ *Singing*

✳ *Travel*

Love is also important to the healing process. The late Smiley Blanton, a psychiatrist and speech pathologist affiliated with Reverend Norman Vincent Peale, said: "Every act committed without the creative power of love implements the degenerative process at work in the body. It is probably true that more people are sick from lack of love in their lives than from all other causes put together."

Bunny Love

In 1980, researchers at the Ohio State University School of Medicine studied the effects of cholesterol, and rabbits were chosen to be fed a high-cholesterol diet. However, the negative effects in one group were significantly lower than the overall group. The researchers discovered that the person who fed that group did not just throw the food into the cages. Rather, he took the rabbits out of their cages and petted, hugged, and kissed them during their feeding. The result was that the rabbits were healthier.

❋ *You are an expression of love, being able to give and receive it. Take some time each day to be still and commune with the love that is the Spirit. This love infuses your mind and body, and heals and restores your entire being. Experience love today with any of the following:*

❋ *Do a kindness for someone without expecting anything in return.*

❋ *Look in the mirror and say, "I love you. I really, really do."*

❋ *Look for a special strength in a friend and tell them what you see.*

❋ *Repeat three times out loud, "I am loved, loveable, and loving."*

❋ *Give a sincere compliment to a spouse, friend, or co-worker within thirty seconds of seeing them.*

❋ *Choose one quality, skill, or personality trait you like about yourself, and be grateful.*

❋ *Give a stranger a big smile.*

❋ *Look in the mirror and give yourself a big smile.*

❋ *Speak lovingly to a cat, dog, or small child.*

❋ *Give yourself thirty minutes to an hour for a fun activity that you like.*

Express love and appreciation for every organ and part of your physical body. For example, say to your heart: "I love and appreciate my heart because it is constantly pumping blood, carrying nutrients and oxygen throughout my body." After appreciating every part you can think of, you will once again realize what a wonderful vehicle your body is.

If you think of your body as a Rolls Royce, you can then imagine how special you are, the spiritual you, living in that body. You deserve wholeness.

Step Six Exercises

1. *A technique of forgiveness is to become quiet, and repeat a prayer or read an inspiring passage from a spiritual text. Say: "I fully forgive (name) and let him or her go into the hands of Spirit. That incident is in the past and I now choose to release its hold on me. I wish him or her well in all their endeavors. I allow the power of Spirit to sever all negativity between us. I am free, and he or she is free."*

2. *Visualize a rope connecting you with the other person. Get the sense that a beam of white light cuts the rope that binds you. See yourself and the other person enfolded in white light, healing all resentment and freeing you both to move forward with your lives.*

3. *Whenever you think of the person or the past incident, take a moment to bless the other person with thoughts of goodwill and then switch your mind to something else. In time you will be completely free from the feelings that have held you back.*

Step Seven

Super Abundance

*"Give, and it shall be given unto you.... For
with the same measure that ye mete withal it shall
be measured to you again."*
—Luke 6:38

What is abundance? For many, money comes to mind. Others grapple with the centuries-old confusion that spirituality requires financial poverty. Some equate abundance with successful relationships or world travel.

To me, *abundance is having what I need and more when I need it.* Abundance is a shift in consciousness that is available to all of us. It is a firm belief in Spirit, the Spiritual Self, and its unwavering ability to provide us with the good our hearts desire.

The notion of abundance is comprehended when you see your life as a purpose-filled mission, which, when fulfilled, brings you abundance almost automatically.

Divine Tailoring

Kimberley came to me for counseling. She had just moved to Manhattan from another state and due to unforeseen circumstances, her plans of staying with a friend were cut short. She had no place to stay the following night. Kimberley explained that she had only a few leads for possible places to live and did not have enough money for a long-term lease.

A fashion designer by trade, Kimberley had been inspired by the story of a businessman who took God as his partner and went on to create a very successful business bearing the name of Spirit and his own. Kimberley also wanted God as her partner. In our meeting, we talked about Spirit as the source of what she needed.

She turned her attention from the lack of needing an apartment and turned within to Source, her Spiritual Self. We recited an affirmation together from Paramhansa Yogananda: "I will go forth in perfect faith in the power of omnipresent good to bring me what I need at the time that I need it." Kimberley left our meeting feeling confident and hopeful that with the support of Spirit, she would find a place to live.

That afternoon, she walked through the streets of Manhattan looking for an apartment and silently repeated the affirmation. The next day she called me from an apartment on Fifth Avenue that she had rented for two months.

"Remember the story of the businessman who took God as his partner?" she asked. "Well, outside my window I can see the sign from the business he started: *Lord and Taylor*."

A few days later she sent me a box of candy from Lord and Taylor with a note saying, "Truly, the Lord is my tailor." Though we later discovered that the Lord and Taylor story was a myth, I believe that Spirit used the story to inspire Kimberley.

We have all received the inheritance of the kingdom of possibilities within. You are an expression of Source, with at least one unique gift to share with the world. The Spiritual Self nudges you from within, urging you to use your gifts. When you are willing and open, you begin to receive ideas about how you can best use your talents. The nudges from Spirit come through your daydreams and also from what you enjoy doing so much that you would do it without being paid.

* *Listen to the urges within yourself. What do you want to do? How do you want to express your self?*

* *In a notebook or journal, write down three things that you really want. Do this for one week without looking at what you wrote the previous day. At the end of the week, read the entries and pursue the things most often repeated.*

* *Take up clowning.*

* *Learn salsa dancing.*

* *Learn woodworking.*

* *Start your own business.*

* *Learn public speaking.*

* *Volunteer at a hospital.*

* *Take an auto mechanic course.*

* *Volunteer for a cause you believe in.*

Maybe you have spent your life trying to live up to expectations or meet the needs of others, and lost sight of your own desires and dreams. It is important to accept that you are a unique **expression of God, and that you deserve to receive your inheritance of abundant good.** You were created to know and express the unique expression of Spirit that you are.

This chapter shows you how to claim your inheritance of infinite supply for living a life of security and wellbeing as you fulfill your unique mission in the world.

Manifest True Abundance

Abundance is usually thought of as the manifestation of jobs, things, or money. While those things are certainly important, pursuing them for their own sake cannot lead to true abundance. You want them in the first place so that you can feel peace and happiness or other sense of wellbeing. Instead of pursuing material wealth, thinking that will bring an elevated state of being, I have found a formula that has manifested *true* abundance.

There are many examples of people who have made money their god, and paid the price of public embarrassment, ruined health, and strained relationships. However, money is not the root of evil. *There isn't anything wrong with money or having lots of it. Depend on Spirit, not money, as the source of your supply.* If you are dependent on money, things, or jobs for your security and wellbeing, then your security will waver when these change.

Making money for money's sake is not the way to achieve true peace and happiness. Making money to live well and fulfill your mission and bless others are great reasons for seeking financial prosperity.

Listen to your inner guidance and follow that first; as a result you will have what you need when you need them and more.

One of Spirit's blessings in my life has been working with a physical trainer who works with some of the top Professional Golfers' Association players in the United States. My body has been transformed as a result. At the end of a recent training session, my friend and I sat on the porch of a five-star resort clubhouse, sipping our drinks as we looked out on a marsh view while a man played bagpipes on the manicured lawn. We felt richly blessed for the luxurious experience. Putting Spirit first in my life through the years has resulted in many experiences that could only come from Spirit's hand in my life.

Opening Doors

In January 1998, I resided at Ananda Meditation Retreat and lived on about $600 a month. I was very contented. It was a life-transforming experience that gave me invaluable tools for spiritual growth.

I started to have nudges from Spirit after three years. I needed a change to keep living my mission. Spirit implanted in me the desire to concentrate more fully on my public speaking. With that came the desire to earn a higher income.

In February 1999, I set a six-month goal to earn a thousand dollars a month through my speaking. A month later I was offered an associate minister position to Eric Butterworth. In two months I spoke to hundreds of people each week at Lincoln Center and earned more than three times what I had set as the goal. When the time was right, and when I truly listened to Spirit's guidance, the doors opened.

Five years later, Source let me know again that it was time for a new adventure.

Spirit will also let you know when it's time to re-examine your current situation, go within for guidance, and listen for a new course of action.

When I use my natural talents in a way that also benefits others, I experience a deep sense of peace and happiness. For instance, I enjoy reading inspiring books and sharing what I learn through writing and speaking. In this process I experience abundance, and when I receive something in return, it is like icing on the cake.

What unique talents is your Spiritual Self urging you to put into expression? What needs are there in the world that using your talents would fill?

* *Public speaking: Inspirational-motivational speaker for non-profit groups*

* *Carpentry skills: Volunteer with Habitat for Humanity*

* *Medical training: Volunteer with Doctors without Borders*

* *Writing: Write and publish how-to or inspirational books*

* *Accounting: Treasurer for a non-profit organization*

* *Swimming: Teach physically challenged children or adults*

* *Golf: Teach children how to play*

Kick-Start Abundance Through Giving

While it may sound paradoxical, abundance is set into motion when you engage in the act of giving. When in your consciousness you feel you have more than enough and can share your good with others, you are mirroring abundance.

There are many ways to practice giving. You give to Source every time you pray and meditate, study spiritual principles, or spend time with like-minded people. You give when you do your very best in whatever work or activity you are engaged in. You give when you go out of our way to help another person, without attachment to the result.

Unexpected Blessings

Mehdi, an insurance company's top agent, visited a policyholder suffering from heart disease who wanted to file a claim. There wasn't any hope of selling him more insurance.

Most agents would have probably given him the form and left. But Mehdi not only assisted him in filling out the form, but—on finding out that the man had other insurers—helped him get the other forms and fill them out as well. Further, he ensured that pending refunds came through. Mehdi would not accept payment for his help.

A few days later he received through the mail a list of twenty-one of the man's relatives and friends, names, dates of birth, number of children, and additional personal history about each one. Mehdi sold millions of dollars of insurance to them. Giving without expectation of anything in return opened up a way for abundance to flow into Mehdi's life.

It is easy to give when you know you are going to get something tangible in return. However, abundance is achieved by *giving without expectation.* Had Mehdi just done what was in his job description, he would have received his weekly payroll check as usual. But when he gave more of his talents without expectation, he was blessed with abundance.

The act of giving unlocks the joy of your spiritual nature and gives you a sense of being an integral part of a giving, abundant Universe. Can you remember when you did something for someone without any strings attached and felt overwhelming love and joy as a result? When you give for the joy of giving, you are operating from the Spiritual Self.

✸ *How much should you give to put the cycle of abundance into motion? Where is the boundary between giving and depleting your energy? The right gauge is to give as long as you feel joy and are guided to give. Rely on your inner guidance as to how, when, and to what degree you give of yourself. On a scale of 1 to 10 (the highest being 10), rank how much you enjoy and find satisfaction in the following activities.*

✸ *Ushering or welcoming people in your church.*

✸ *Helping urban youth.*

✸ *Calling or visiting family members.*

✸ *Serving on the board of a non-profit organization.*

✸ *Volunteering in a club.*

You are given unique gifts and talents, and the opportunity to express them and make a difference in the world. As a result you will be blessed with an abundance of good.

Along with giving of one's self, an important spiritual practice is to give financial support to charities, churches, or other organizations or individuals that support Spirit's work in the world. You learn what you really believe by what you do with your money.

Mark Victor Hansen, coauthor of *Chicken Soup for the Soul,* writes that tithing will multiply money, not subtract. "It expands, multiplies, and adds value to all that you do. When you begin to live this law, you'll lay claim to a multiplied harvest of thirty-fold, sixty-fold, or one hundred-fold."

The late Sir John Marks Templeton, founder of the Templeton Fund, said, "Tithing always gives the greatest return on your investment." Other notable people who have tithed their way to abundance are John D. Rockefeller, Andrew Carnegie, and Oprah Winfrey. These individuals attributed their prosperity to the practice of tithing, and, of course, to giving expression to their talents.

Learn to give without attachment to the result. Perhaps this is why Jesus said, "…let not thy left hand know what thy right hand doeth." (Matthew 6:3) He was saying to give without an expectation of a return. Give for the joy of giving. Give because you are grateful for the blessings already received. Give to express and affirm your faith. Give because it makes you feel terrific about yourself and the difference you are making.

Good News

Hall of Fame golfer Roberto De Vicenzo had just received a check for winning first place in a golf tournament. While in the parking lot, a woman approached him and became emotional about her son who was very sick and that she didn't have the money to pay for the treatment he required. Roberto signed over his check to this woman.

Later, someone said to Roberto, "That lady has approached others with the same false story about her son. You were scammed." Roberto responded, "You mean there isn't a young child suffering from a life-threatening illness? What a relief. Thank God." With his generous heart, Roberto was truly rich and living the life of abundance.

Get a Bigger Receptacle and Be a Good Receiver

I spoke with a woman who did not feel worthy to experience the presence of God. I explained that feeling the presence is not something that we have to earn. It is a free gift. All that matters is our willingness to know Source by tapping into our Spiritual Self.

Spirit is more than willing to pour into our consciousness if we are open to receive. *We are children of God, and heirs to all that is necessary for fulfillment and joy.* Usually a child's needs are met without the child having to worry about them. The child is given food, clothing, an education, and even paid vacations. If the children of earthly parents are taken care of so well, then as a child of God we should feel entitled to be taken care of on an even greater scale.

The wife of a man from the company of the prophets had lost her husband, and her creditors were going to take away her children in payment for a debt. Elisha, a superhero of the Bible, visited and asked her what she had in her house. She said, "Thine handmaid hath not any thing in the house, save a pot of oil." (2 Kings 4:2) Elisha said to her: "Go, borrow thee vessels abroad of all thy neighbors, even empty vessels; borrow not a few." (2 Kings 4:3) He asked her to pour the oil into as many containers as she could. The oil flowed continuously as she filled every container that she had. When she had no more containers, the oil stopped flowing.

🌸 *We are only able to receive as much as we can accept. The bigger our containers, the more we can receive. How big is the container of your consciousness? What do you imagine experiencing in your life in terms of abundance? Circle what is important in your life.*

🌸 *Doing work you love.*

🌸 *Owning your own business.*

🌸 *Spending time with friends.*

🌸 *Being married.*

🌸 *Owning a pet.*

🌸 *Going on a tropical vacation.*

🌸 *Owning a new car.*

🌸 *Owning your own home.*

🌸 *Earning enough money so that you are no longer fearful about paying bills.*

🌸 *Being your ideal weight.*

🌸 *Eating nutritious and tasty food.*

🌸 *Eating in restaurants.*

🌸 *Playing golf or tennis once or more times per week.*

🌸 *Saving enough money to retire at age seventy-five and live comfortably for thirty more years.*

✳ *Spending time with grandchildren.*

✳ *Taking a yoga class or getting a massage.*

✳ *Spending time in meditation daily.*

✳ *Being part of a spiritual community.*

Riding First Class

A Russian peasant who lived in a small village had to travel to Moscow. He had never been to the metropolis, and wondered how he would get there. Neighbors instructed him that a train station could be found a few towns over, and he would have to ride the train to get to the country's capital. He had never been aboard a train and hoped that all would go well.

Having walked twenty miles to the train station, he was directed to the ticket window. Not realizing he had a choice, he bought a first-class ticket. Then he waited for the train, lining up behind other passengers whose actions he hoped to imitate.

The train arrived, and those in front of him ran to the back of the train and hid under seats. A bit puzzled, he did the same, not very successfully. The conductor walked by and pulled him from under the seat: "Where do you think you are going without a ticket?"

"But I have one," pleaded the peasant as he showed the conductor his ticket.

Examining it, the conductor exclaimed, "This is a ticket

for first class. In addition to the comfort and luxury of the ride, you also get served three meals a day. Why are you riding in third class, and under the seat?"

"I had no idea what to do, so I followed whatever the other people did," replied the peasant.

The conductor laughed: "The others have no tickets so they hide to avoid being caught. But you, with your first-class ticket, should be traveling in luxury and comfort."

Many of us are riding underneath car seats with first-class tickets, living our lives without remembering that we are children of Spirit that is omnipotent, limitless, and wants the very best for us. You can change this false notion today.

Many of us have forgotten who we are. We are expressions of God, with the inheritance of all that is good. As a result of our poor memory, we have traveled under the seat in the back of the train. You are born with a first-class ticket, and if you don't believe it, at least act as if you do. Eventually, you will believe.

Paramhansa **Yogananda writes, "Think of divine abundance as a mighty, refreshing rain; whatever receptacle we have at hand will receive it. If you hold a tin cup, you will receive only that quantity. If you hold up a bowl, that will be filled. What kind of receptacle are you holding up to divine abundance?"**

Some people are good givers, but not good receivers. Yet if you want to experience the abundance of God's Kingdom, then you must also be a good receiver of the good that comes your way. When someone offers to give or to do something for you, accept the gift with the knowledge that this is an expression of Spirit. By being a good receiver, you also give to the person who gave to you because you are fulfilling his or her need to give.

Have you ever been excited to give somebody a gift, only to have your excitement lessened when the gift was not accepted well?

* *Note the blessings that unfold in your life each and every day. If someone gives you a gift, buys you lunch, or pays you a compliment, then acknowledge these as abundance in manifestation. Take note of these daily gifts for a period of seven days, and your life will change for the better.*

* *A feeling of gratitude also increases the flow of abundance. Take note of all the things for which you feel grateful, tangible and intangible, instead of focusing on what is missing and watch your consciousness change to a more abundant state. The secret to happiness is satisfaction and gratitude for what you have, the love you receive, and what Source gives you.*

This ... Or Something Better

What happens when we don't get what we think we rightfully desire? Spirit generally has something even better in mind. Sometimes we don't get the desired outcomes because the things that we think we want are not necessarily what we *really* want. To do the work we are called to do, there may be a period of gaining certain life or work experiences.

Better Than Imagined

For five years, I worked in New York City as the associate minister to Eric Butterworth, who passed on during my fourth year there. At first I thought that Spirit's plan for me was to succeed him as the leader of the ministry. But I soon realized that God had something different in mind.

One of my passions is playing golf. I love being outdoors and playing golf is a great way to get away from the intense urban environment. I started to write down things that I desired, one of which was to be in a warmer climate where I could play golf all year long. It wasn't long before I became the new minister at the Unity Church of Hilton Head Island in South Carolina, a golfer's paradise. Hilton Head enjoys moderate, warm weather, has plenty of trees and water, wonderful people and provided me with the opportunity to earn more than I did when I was in New York. As mentioned earlier, I was hired to be the senior minister of the Unity Center of New York exactly seven years later. Now I have the experience necessary to lead the Center to their next level of growth. And *Super You*, which I started work on twelve years ago in New York, was finally published.

Sometimes we do not realize how big our dreams are and that they can become our physical reality. It is important to affirm, "This or something better." While your good is unfolding, remember that your deepest desire and greatest purpose is to be aware of the presence in the moment. You can be content and happy when you focus your attention on being present in this moment and to Source. *A Course in Miracles* says, "Infinite Patience bears immediate results." The immediate results of patience are peace and contentment. Patience is a result of being present to Spirit in the moment.

Have you ever received something in life that you wanted only to realize that it failed to make you happy? King Midas desired to have the golden touch but was tragically disappointed when everything he loved turned to gold, including his wife and children. The apostle Paul said that even if we understand all mysteries and all knowledge and have faith that can move mountains, we are nothing unless we have love. Love never fails.

What is meant by love? Love is empathy for all living creatures, regardless of how they treat us or how unlovable they may seem. Sometimes love is easy, such as the love you experience toward a family member, spouse, partner, or a dear friend. More challenging is the love for those who are not so nice to you. In both cases you must find love within, and express from that place to experience true happiness.

It is possible to love people and not associate with them on a personal level. You can forgive people, love them, and not like them. Love is seeing the whole world through the eyes of right understanding, and realizing that although people often act out of their pain, ultimately everyone wants to love and to be loved.

The Three Old Men

A woman came out of her house and saw three old men with long white beards sitting in her front yard. Since they looked harmless, she invited them into her house.

"We generally don't go into a house together," one replied. "How come?"

"His name is Wealth," the man said, pointing to one of his friends. "He is Success," he added, pointing to the other one. "And I am Love. Please go back inside and check with your family which one of us you would like to come in."

The woman went in and told her husband what was said.

He was overjoyed. "Let us invite Wealth. Let him come and fill our home with riches. Then all our miseries will vanish."

His wife disagreed: "My dear, why don't we invite Success? One can have wealth and yet not be successful."

Their daughter jumped in with her own suggestion: "Would it not be better to invite Love? Our home will be filled with love. Won't that be the best of all?"

After some deliberation, they agreed with their daughter. The woman went out and said to Love: "Please come in and be our guest."

Love got up and started walking toward the house. The other two followed him. Surprised, the lady asked Wealth and Success: "I only invited Love. Why are you coming in?"

Success replied, "If you had just invited Wealth or myself, the other two of us would have stayed out. But since you invited Love, wherever he goes, we go with him. Wherever there is love, there is also wealth and success."

Focus on living from your Spiritual Self of love. Do what you love. Love what you do. Do everything with an attitude of service. When you seek first to know and live in tune with Spirit, you will gain not only the inner happiness and freedom your soul craves but also the outer riches *you deserve.*

Step Seven Exercises

1. *Close your eyes and visualize standing in a meadow with a rain of golden light showering you. As the droplets of golden light descend, experience a sense of joy, calm, and fulfillment. Visualize an abundance receptacle that you're holding. What does your receptacle look like? What color or shape is it? What makes it uniquely yours?*

2. *Think of an aspect of abundance that you would like more of, such as friendship, creative ideas, career success, or money. Visualize the receptacle you are holding getting bigger and bigger, as big as you can comfortably imagine it. Feel the drops of golden light pouring into your receptacle along with symbols of the abundance you desire. Be grateful that everything you need or want for complete fulfillment is now yours. The receptacle represents your consciousness, and the shower of golden light is unlimited abundance. Repeat this visualization anytime you want to remind yourself that the good you are seeking is already yours through the Spirit within.*

3. *For additional resources and support for manifesting true abundance, go to www.superyoubook.com/bookbonus.*

Conclusion

Thank you for taking this journey of discovery to express Super You. This journey to the summit of spiritual awakening is not only very satisfying but also one of the greatest challenges you will ever face.

Knowing God involves letting go of false beliefs that no longer serve you, and developing new ways of thinking and being. The greatest human achievements have required tremendous commitment, desire, and discipline. The journey of knowing and living in tune with Spirit also requires your best intention and effort. This is what Jesus meant when he said, "…love the Lord your God with all your heart, and with all your soul, and with all your mind, and with all your strength." (Mark 12:30)

Don't be discouraged if your progress seems slow. Press on and know that you have many friends around the world taking this journey with you. As you proceed, you will experience more of the fruits and miraculous manifestations in your life.

I hope that you will do more than be inspired and entertained by what you have read, and will daily apply the principles and enjoy the resulting fruits. Many who read a book like this are like those who are over-read and underdone. They have many books but have not thought deeply about what they have read or applied the principles to *their life*. They do not know the truth of what they read but only know *about* it.

Intellectual knowledge is important, but I encourage you to apply the principles you have found in this book to experience your Spiritual Self on a daily basis. Through daily practice and persistence, you will experience the faith, love, joy, and abundance that are within you. It is not the years of reading or hearing lectures *about* God but the present moments of *realizing* and *knowing* Source that will transform your life and our world.

Like the greatest teachers and prophets who have walked among us, you can also live in tune with Spirit. You have in your hands the seven steps for knowing God and living a life of abundance, joy, love, meaning, and purpose.

I would love to hear about how you have applied the principles from this book, or how they have blessed someone else. Write to me at *www.superyoubook.com/bookbonus*.

I look forward to the next time we connect on this greatest of adventures in knowing God and becoming Super You.

God bless you.

Appendix

Meditation for Beginners

This section is divided in two parts, technique and expansion, to be practiced in that order during each meditation session. While technique brings you to that place of stillness within, expansion is where you will feel the joy and tap into ways to experience communion with Spirit.

Technique

Sit Comfortably

Sit in a chair, preferably without arms, or cross-legged on the floor. A chair works best for Westerners who are not used to sitting cross-legged. The advantage of sitting cross-legged is that the energy of your body is in a constant circular flow. However, the chair will do just fine. The most important thing is to keep your spine erect and chin parallel to the floor. Sitting upright enables the energy in your body to more freely flow toward the brain. If you have back problems, make whatever adjustments are necessary such as putting some pillows behind you. *Sitting upright is important to staying awake.*

Place your palms facing upward at the juncture of your thighs and hips. This sends the message to your mind that you are open and receptive to Spirit. Close your eyes. You're now in a position conducive to being still. This position will become comfortable with practice.

Relax Your Body

In meditation, we seek to quiet the mind. Tension in the body creates disturbance in the mind. Relax your body by taking a long, deep breath, tensing every muscle, then throw your breath out and let your body relax. Repeat this three to six times. In this way, you release unwanted tension that you are holding unconsciously.

Breathe in slowly through your nose for a count of five to twenty, depending on your lung capacity. Hold your breath for the same count, and exhale for the same count. For example, you might breathe in for a count of six, hold for six, and exhale for a count of six. This is one round. Do six to twelve rounds to relax your body and calm and energize your mind.

Now scan your body from your feet to the top of your head, mentally sending each muscle the message to relax and let go. There is no need to force your body to relax; trust that your cells are intelligent and will respond to your mental suggestions. If there is a particular area of tension, give it some extra mental attention. Visualize white light enveloping and relaxing it.

After your body is relaxed, try to keep perfectly still. When the body is still, the mind can be still. Eventually these steps will become easy and automatic.

Observe Your Breathing

Once your body is relaxed, become aware of the flow of your breath. Because of the intimate connection between the mind and the breath, use your breath as a tool for quieting the mind and connecting with Spirit. When you observe your breathing, your breath becomes longer and shallower, and your mind is concentrated and calm.

Now observe the flow of your breathing as it moves through the nasal passages. If that is difficult, then observe the rise and fall of your chest as you inhale and exhale. Don't control your breathing, but observe what is already happening. Observe your breath as you would observe the waves rolling in to the shore and then back out to the ocean.

Managing the Wandering Mind

As you observe your breath, your mind will naturally begin to wander. In every workshop on meditation, one of the major concerns is how to stop the wandering mind. The answer is that you don't stop it. What you can do is learn how to manage the mind. *Do not judge yourself for having a roaming mind or for the types of thoughts that go through your mind when you try to get still.*

Rather than resisting, be gentle and firm with your mind. When you notice that your mind has wandered, bring it back to watching your breath. If you have to do this many times, that is natural. The more you practice being still, the less your mind will wander. I once had a student exclaim that this technique of managing his wandering mind was one of the most helpful ideas he had learned in forty years on the spiritual path.

There will be days when your mind is more manageable than others due to the types of experiences you've had or even what you ate that day. No one eliminates the wandering mind altogether, except in moments of deep meditation when the mind becomes completely still on its own. In the meantime, do your best to remain as still and focused as possible.

Mental Repetition

There's a saying in India: *"The mind is like a tree, full of drunken monkeys."* Beyond observing your breath, focus your monkey mind by silently repeating a word or a phrase. For instance, repeat the words "I am" as you inhale and the word "Spirit" as you exhale. For the word, "Spirit," substitute any word that inspires you, such as "peace," "love," "joy," "God," or "Om." Stick to one word or phrase during each meditation session.

This phase of meditation should be done for one-quarter of the time you have allotted for meditation. If you are meditating for eight minutes, do this phase for two. Remember, the mind is going to wander. When it does, gently but firmly bring your thoughts back to the breath and/or repeating the word or phrase.

Expansion

After you have relaxed your body, watched your breath, and concentrated on the word or phrase for a period of time, let go of the technique and choose one of the following options for expansion. The technique has quieted your mind, and your heart has opened up. *You are knocking at the door of your secret hideout and receptive to being ushered into the secret chamber* where you can experience Spirit and get in touch with your Spiritual Self.

Following are several options for expansion you can experiment with during your meditation sessions. You can practice one or more during any session.

Becoming Aware of the Heart's Feeling

If you relate particularly to the realm of emotions (although this is not a limiting criterion), choose your heart area as your point of focus and be receptive to whatever feelings are there. Don't try to make yourself feel anything, just notice if you do. There might be feelings of peace, joy, love, or calmness.

We are often not aware of these feelings because of our restless monkey minds. **When your mind is calm, your heart opens up and these feelings emerge.** Let your mind become absorbed in whatever feeling is present in your heart. Unpleasant emotions may also emerge from past hurts. Try not to be alarmed by them. They are manifesting themselves to you to be acknowledged and healed; reread step one, Super Acceptance, to support you.

Focusing on Your Third Eye

To focus your attention during this phase of meditation, particularly if you enjoy being in your intellect, is to gaze deeply (with closed eyes) at the point between the eyebrows. Many call this the third eye. The third eye is a subtle energy center through which you can access intuitive knowledge. This is also the location of the prefrontal lobes, the source of positive emotions and behaviors.

When you are very still in meditation, you might see fragments of your third eye, or the whole eye at once. Or you may not see anything. I have seen parts of the spiritual eye but never its entirety, and frequently do not see any part. Whether you actually see the third eye or not is not a measure of how far along on the spiritual path you are or how well you are meditating. You do not need to see it to feel it drawing you deeper within.

Listening to Inner Sounds

Another way you can focus in this phase of meditation, particularly if you prefer using your auditory faculty, is by listening to inner sounds. For thousands of years, Indian spiritual masters have taught that there is a subtle body within our physical body. This subtle body contains seven energy centers known as chakras.

Each chakra regulates the flow of spiritual energy in the body and influences the organs nearest the chakra. Chakras are located at the base of the spine, the reproductive organs, the navel, the heart, the throat, the point between the eyebrows, and the crown of the head. Each chakra vibrates to create a sound that can be heard in meditation. The sounds include water in a stream, crickets, a bell, string instruments such as a harp, wind blowing in the trees, a flute, and the crash of ocean waves.

Just as with seeing the third eye, you may not hear anything. If you do hear a sound, listen and allow it to transport you deeper within. If you don't hear anything when you decide to listen, focus on another aspect of expansion and listen again at another time.

Visualizing

Visualizing a desired outcome programs your mind to help you achieve it. If you consider yourself particularly visual, you may be drawn to this method of expansion. See your self performing an activity or achieving a goal in as much detail as possible. If you want to improve a skill, see yourself performing that skill in an excellent fashion. If you want to achieve a certain goal, imagine yourself already having achieved it. See your self play-ing the piano, giving a speech, closing a sale, getting an A on an exam, or meeting your life companion.

Asking for Guidance

You might want to ask Spirit a question in order to receive the answer or solution to a problem. Ask the question with your focus at the point between the eyebrows and listen for a response within your heart. If you do not receive the answer at this time, trust that you will receive what you need to know at the right time and in the right way. See step four, Living in the Super Zone, to gain more insights on discerning spiritual guidance.

Talking to God/Spirit

If the idea resonates with you, *have a conversation with God or Spirit.* Talk to God or Spirit about your desires, concerns, or whatever else you are inspired to talk about.

Praying for Others

Be an instrument for others during meditation by allowing the spiritual energy that you contact to flow through you as a blessing to someone else. Visualize the person you are praying for as being filled with a brilliant white light, trusting that he or she is blessed with whatever it is that is needed the most at this time. Visualize the person smiling, with a peaceful and lov-ing countenance, or looking healthy and strong and filled with vitality. By visualizing the expression of positive qualities, you are supporting a greater expression of his or her Spiritual Self.

Another practice of praying for others—and a great way to end your meditation time—is to rub your hands together, making them instruments for energy to flow through. Hold your hands about shoulder height with palms facing frontward. Chant "Om" three times or choose a different sacred word. Feel the spiritual energy flowing through your palms as a blessing to everyone you are praying for.

After Meditating

Gradually move your awareness back to your body and surrounding environment. You may want to take a few long, slow, deep breaths. Be aware of the sounds around you. Feel the chair and floor beneath you. Wiggle your toes and fingers and move your body gently. Slowly open your eyes and adjust to the lighting.

Note if any message comes up for you during the expansion portion of your meditation session. Is there something you feel compelled to do, or is there a person you should talk to? Did you receive an exciting new idea or get a solution to a problem? Perhaps nothing came up for you. That's okay. Getting a message is not the point of meditating, merely a by-product. The point is to experience that deep peace and joy within, thereby contacting the spiritual presence in you. If your meditation is unpleasant for any reason, remain persistent, and eventually you will begin to reap the fruits.

Bring whatever peace or joy you experience into your daily activities. Instead of jumping out of your chair and shouting, "I've got to get the kids up, take a shower, walk the dog, pack a lunch, and make it to the bus," transition slowly into your day. Do something simple and physical first, like unloading the dishwasher, making the bed, or taking a shower.

A Young Yogi Re-Enters

In his classic, *Autobiography of a Yogi*, Paramhansa Yogananda tells about his first experience of a very deep state of meditation. Immediately after, his teacher handed him a broom and they began to sweep the porch. His teacher wanted him to be able to bring his experience into his daily life.

Making Meditation a Habit

Many people get excited about meditation, practice it a few times, and then fall out of the habit. It is important to make meditation a habit to experience the benefits. The neophyte in meditation will need to practice several times before the benefits become tangible. Here are some tips for making meditation a daily habit so that you will do it easily and automatically. In fact, like not brushing your teeth, eventually you will feel uncomfortable when you don't meditate.

Best Times to Meditate

The best times to meditate are first thing in the morning, before any distractions catch your attention, and in the evening, preferably at sunset or before going to bed. The most important thing is to find whatever time works best for you. *I have had some very blissful meditation periods riding on a bus during rush hour in New York City.*

Meditate before you eat, or two to three hours later. Your body uses energy to digest food, and you want that energy available for meditation. I like to meditate before breakfast and before going to bed. Choose a time that works best for your schedule and adjust it as necessary. In the beginning, you may not be able to meditate twice a day, so choose one time in the morning or evening.

How Long?

Meditate as long as you feel joy, and then a little longer. This might mean only a few minutes at first. Purchase a non-ticking countdown timer to set for the time you have allotted to meditate, even if it's for a few minutes.

End your meditation period looking forward to the next time. Start with short periods and build up from there. A long-term goal might be to meditate for thirty minutes twice a day, morning and evening. I started meditating three minutes a day in 1985. Now I am up to an hour and a half to two hours a day. However, don't compare your practice to anyone else's. Make this process as enjoyable as possible so that you will be in it for the long haul.

The quality of your time is more important than the quantity. The soul loves to meditate, but the ego resists it. If you are persistent in your practice, eventually you will look forward to it every day.

Light Exercise

Be awake and energized when you meditate. If you feel lethargic when you sit down for your session, do some kind of exercise to get your energy flowing. The more physically fit you are, the easier it will be for your body to sit still without aches and pains. *In yoga philosophy, the primary reason for doing postures, or asanas, is so that the body can be comfortable and fluid during meditation.*

Creating a Sacred Space

Find a special place in your home for your meditation practice. Take a special chair and pick out a corner of your home where all you do is meditate. Then whenever you sit down in that chair, you will automatically begin to feel like meditating. The *energy from your meditation space will have a positive influence on everyone who lives in or enters your home.*

Setting Up an Altar

Set up an altar in your sacred space where you can put objects that will inspire you to meditate. This includes pictures of your family, spiritual figures like Buddha, Jesus, Krishna, or anything that inspires you. Place fresh flowers on the altar and/or light a candle as you begin. The goal is to create something that you enjoy sitting in front of that elevates and inspires you.

Blocking Out Sounds

Meditate in the quietest location you can find in your home. Earplugs or headphones can help dampen any noise. You want to block out distractions as much as possible to tune into your secret hideout. With practice, you will be able to meditate anywhere, regardless of how much noise is in the environment.

Stay Warm and Comfortable

Meditate in a room that is on the cool side to stay refreshed and awake. Your body temperature will drop as you meditate. You may want a small blanket available or dress in warm, comfortable clothing.

Meditating in a Group

While you will benefit from meditating alone, join a group for this practice about once a week. *There is a concentration of energy in a group meditating together.* If there are people in the group who have been meditating for years, their consciousness will help you. People have reported that meditating with others has enabled them to establish a high level of understanding and special rapport with those who shared in their meditations.

Meditating Longer

Make one of your goals to double your meditation time once a week. If you regularly meditate five minutes per day, then meditate for ten minutes once a week. This will help stretch your ability.

For more information on how you can deepen your meditation practice and receive additional support, scan the QR code below or log on to *www.superyoubook.com/bookbonus*.

May your meditation practice bring you much joy and profound peace.

Sources and Further Reading

_____. *The Holy Bible,* King James version.

_____. *A Course in Miracles.* Huntington Station, NY: Foundation for Inner Peace, 1975.

Albom, Mitch. *Have a Little Faith.* New York: Hyperion, 2009.

Amos, Wally. *The Power In You.* New York, E. P. Dutton, 1988.

de Avila, Saint Theresa. *The Autobiography of St. Teresa of Avila: The Life of St. Teresa of Jesus.* Charlotte, NC: TAN Books and Publishers, 2009.

Butterworth, Eric. *Spiritual Prosperity,* third edition. Unity Village, MO: Unity House, 2001.

_____. *The Creative Life.* New York: Tarcher, 2001.

Byrne, Rhonda. *The Secret.* Hillsboro, OR: Atria Books/ Beyond Words, 2006.

Canfield, Jack, and Mark Victor Hansen. *Chicken Soup for the Soul.* Deerfield Beach, FL: Health Communications Inc., 2001

Carnegie, Dale. *How to Win Friends and Influence People.* Reissue edition. New York: Simon & Schuster, 2009.

de Chardin, Pierre Teilhard. *The Heart of the Matter.* New York: Mariner Books, 2002.

Coffee, Captain Gerald. *Beyond Survival.* New York: G. P. Putnam, 1990.

Covey, Stephen. *First Things First.* New York: Simon & Schuster, 1994.

Douillard, John. *Body, Mind, and Sport.* New York: Harmony Books, 1994.

Fillmore, Charles, and Jim Gaither. *The Essential Charles Fillmore: Collected Writings of a Missouri Mystic.* Unity Village, MO: Unity House, 1999.

Fox, Emmet. *Around the Year with Emmet Fox,* second edition. New York: HarperOne, 1992

Frankl, Viktor. *Man's Search for Meaning.* Boston, MA: Beacon Press, 2006.

Gallwey, W. Timothy. *The Inner Game of Golf.* New York: Random House, 1998.

Gans, Danny with R.G. Ryan. *The Voices in My Head.* Las Vegas, NV: Stephens Press, 2009.

Hanh, Thich Nhat. *Peace Is Every Step.* New York: Bantam Books, 1991.

Hawkins, Dr. David R. *Power vs. Force.* West Sedona, AZ: Veritas Publishing, 1995.

James, William. *Varieties of Religious Experience.* New York: Cosimo Classics, 2007.

Kelley, Tim. *True Purpose.* Berkeley, CA: Transcendental Solutions Press, 2009.

Laubach, Frank. *Letters by a Modern Mystic.* Colorado Springs, CO: Purposeful Design Publications, 2007.

Leopardi, Giacomo. *Canti: Poems, A Bilingual Edition* translated by Jonathan Galassi. New York: Farrar, Straus and Giroux, 2010.

Loehr, Jim, and Tony Schwartz. *The Power of Full Engagement.* New York: Free Press, 2004.

Maas, Dr. James B. *Power Sleep.* New York: Villard Books, 1998.

Beth Leilani Mercado Ph.D. , *Whispers of the Soul.* Parker, CO: Outskirts Press, Inc., 2012.

Mitchell, Stephen. *Bhagavad Gita: A New Translation.* New York: Harmony Books, 2002.

Muktananda, Swami. *Play of Consciousness: A Spiritual Autobiography,* third edition. South Fallsburg, NY: Siddha Yoga Publications, 2000.

Peale, Norman Vincent. *The Power of Positive Thinking.* New York: Simon & Schuster, 1994.

Remen, Dr. Rachel Naomi. *The Human Patient.* New York, Anchor Doubleday, 1980.

Roper, Bill. *Compassionate Warrior.* Bloomington, IN: Balboa Press, 2013.

Rosemergy, Jim. *The Sacred Human.* Charleston, SC: Book-Surge Publishing, 2007.

de Sales, Saint Francis. *Treatise on the Love of God.* New York: Cosimo Classics, 2007.

Satchidananda, Sri Swami. *To Know Your Self: The Essential Teachings of Swami Satchidananda,* Second Edition. Buckingham, VA: Integral Yoga Publications, 2008.

Scheinfeld, Robert. *Busting Loose from the Money Game.* Hoboken, NJ: John Wiley, 2006.

Saraswati, Swami Sivananda. *Bliss Divine.* Uttaranchal, India: Divine Life Society, 1997.

Tolle, Eckhart. *A New Earth.* New York: E. P. Dutton, 2005.

Tzu, Lao. *Tao Te Ching,* translated by Jane English and Gia-Fu Feng. New York: Random House, 1974.

Walters, J. Donald. *The Promise of Immortality.* Nevada City, CA: Crystal Clarity Publishers, 2001.

Walters, J. Donald. *The Path,* second edition. Nevada City, CA: Crystal Clarity Publishers, 2004.

Williamson, Marianne. *Return to Love: Reflections on the Principles of* A Course in Miracles. New York: HarperCollins 1992.

Yogananda, Paramhansa. *Autobiography of a Yogi,* thirteenth edition. Los Angeles, CA: Self-realization Fellowship, 2000.

About the Author

Justin Epstein integrates insights from both East and West including Christianity, Yoga philosophy, psychology, science, and personal development, and is a dynamic inspirational speaker who has given over one hundred and thirty presentations to thousands of people in Lincoln Center's Avery Fisher Hall. As a dynamic motivational speaker, he has shared the stage with such notables as Dr. Maya Angelou, Les Brown, Iyanla Vanzant, and Marianne Williamson. Justin has spoken to hundreds of people across the country and for companies such as New York's Roosevelt Hospital and Pop Sustainability.

He graduated *magna cum laude* from James Madison University, where he received a BS degree and double-majored in Communications and Religion/Philosophy, and from Unity Institute in Missouri. After being ordained a Unity Minister in 1993, Justin resided for three and a half years at Ananda Village, a school of Eastern thought.

Justin wrote a newspaper column "Practical Spirituality" for seven years, and is the author of many audiotapes, including the program *The Enlightened Golfer: Merging Mind, Body and Spirit Through the Game.* He produced and hosted the cable television series, "Practical Spirituality," that aired in Manhattan and Brooklyn while he served as the associate to author and speaker Eric Butterworth.

He is also a graduate of the American Comedy Institute and has performed stand-up comedy in clubs throughout New York City including Caroline's on Broadway. Justin is the president/CEO of Justin Epstein International, offering seminars on "The Enlightened Golfer" and also "The Enlightened Leader." Justin is the senior minister of the Unity Center of New York City. He lives in New York.

For additional spiritual support go to
www.superyoubook.com/bookbonus